St. Stephen's Church

Port Washington, N. Y.

St. Stephen's Church

Port Washington, N. Y.

THE INFLUENCE OF PURITANISM

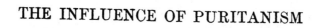

THE INFLUENCE
OF PURITANISM
ON THE POLITICAL & RELIGIOUS
THOUGHT OF THE ENGLISH

BY

JOHN STEPHEN FLYNN

"If Puritanism did not fashion an Apollo with the bow, or a Venus with the apple, it fashioned virile Englishmen."—
DOWDEN.

KENNIKAT PRESS
Port Washington, N. Y./London

THE INFLUENCE OF PURITANISM

First published in 1920
Reissued in 1970 by Kennikat Press
Library of Congress Catalog Card No: 72-102569
SBN 8046-0729-X

Manufactured by Taylor Publishing Company   Dallas, Texas

To those descendants of our Puritan Fathers, in the British Empire and America, who uphold the causes of political and Religious Freedom, for which Puritanism in the seventeenth century ventured all, and who in the crisis of the Great War, with an unquenchable Faith in their ideals and the justice of their cause, bore a noble part in rallying the democracies of both countries to Victory, and in uniting them in a lasting bond of Peace and Friendship, this work is gratefully dedicated.

PREFACE

THE sketches here presented to the reader are of an impressional rather than of an historical character. They are an attempt at an appreciation of tendencies, making for righteousness and freedom, which have taken deep root in the English mind, and changed from time to time the course of politics and the outlook of churches. But while there is no elaboration of historical detail, and no observance of chronological order, history has not been disregarded. So far from that being the case, the period with which we are here most concerned has been carefully re-examined in such authorities as de Rapin and Neale amongst the earlier, and Macaulay and Green amongst the later writers. Traill's "Social England" and Gardiner's "History of the Commonwealth" have been freely used, while general literature on the subject, by both English and American writers, has been consulted at the British Museum. Through the courtesy of Viscount Clifden several little-known political pamphlets of the period have been examined in his library, which contains a good collection of Commonwealth literature. Baxter's "Self Review," with Sir James Stephen's

Essay on Baxter, and Balleine's admirable "History
of the Evangelical Party," "The Journal of John
Wesley," and Ryle's "Christian Leaders of the
Eighteenth Century," throw much light on the
earlier and later phases of the movement.

Morley, Harrison and Carlyle speak for Cromwell; Tuke and Gurney for the Quakers, and
Stoughton for the Independents. Coulton's
"Medieval Studies" (first series) have given valuable information. For America, reliance has been
placed on Professor Max Farrand's "Development
of the United States" and C. Chesterton's "History
of the United States," and for the lighter side of
Puritanism, where the clash of armies and the
wranglings of politicians and sectaries are not
heard, Professor Dowden's "Puritan and Anglican" has met every need. These have been the
chief sources drawn upon for this work.

Yet it would have been quite impossible to have
got at the Puritan mind of the seventeenth century
without such aid as is afforded by Milton's tracts,
Butler's "Hudibras," Lucy Hutchinson's
"Memoirs" of her husband, and Bunyan's
"Pilgrim" and "The Holy War." In these works,
much more really than in the pages of Clarendon
and Burnet, breathes the true Puritan spirit.
The Hudibras is, of course, a caricature, but a
very informing one, and with it Pepys and Selden's
"Table Talk" have been availed of for their
sidelights on the party and the times.

With all this literary wealth ready to hand, the appearance of a new work on Puritanism might seem an impertinence, and, indeed, would be had there been no need of a fresh treatment of the subject, presenting the movement in a juster light than that in which it commonly appears, and relating it to the present age. To trace Puritanism through the many stages of its progress; to show that its light, though often dimmed, has never failed; to distinguish its permanent from its merely transitory elements; to offer proof of the marvellous moral power inherent in it, which enabled it to determine in large measure the character of the great American Republic, as well as to effect many changes in that of the English people; to regard it in the bestowal of wholesome laws, colouring religious thought, educating public opinion, protesting against the popular fallacy that a State has no conscience—this in short is the aim of the present modest work, which the author hopes may, by its brevity and the popular style in which he has tried to cast it, commend itself to many readers who might be repelled by a more exhaustive and ponderous treatise.

Puritanism, often at war with itself and giving birth, from time to time, to rival sects and rival theories of Church and State, possessed a soul unaffected by all these mutations, and independent of circumstances of time and place. In the passing of the years it has shed many of its earlier habits and many visionary and unattainable ideas ; but it has kept its soul. And what manner of soul it is must be judged by what Puritanism has effected in the Evangelical Churches of Christendom, in the political outlook 'of English-speaking peoples, in the Chancelleries of Europe, and in the common life of man, civilised and savage.

J. S. F.

St. John's Lodge,
    Hove, Sussex.

CONTENTS

THE INFLUENCE OF PURITANISM

CHAPTER I

REVIEW OF PURITANISM

To an inquirer into the history of the English people, both at home and overseas, many points of resemblance will be discovered between the ethnological and the moral growth of the race. The student of ethnology finds that many and varied elements have gone to make the Englishman of to-day. If, as some aver, the first of many strata was a branch of the Basques, the upper stratum was undoubtedly Norman; and into this very mixed race there has been flowing silently and almost imperceptibly, through the centuries, many a little rivulet from various European and Eastern sources. The hardy Englishman or Britisher is therefore by no means simplex, a being sprung fresh and pure from English soil, owing nothing to the rest of mankind; for, as a matter of fact, he may track his life-blood to many a parent lake, and is a heavy debtor both to East and West. Nor may we assume that in this respect

1

he has yet reached maturity. The alien still finds England a congenial place, and England appears to be willing enough, after a few futile protests, to absorb and naturalise him. Whether this circumstance is sufficient to account for his unsurpassed success as a coloniser, adapting him to all climates and putting him at ease with all peoples, is a subject which lies somewhat outside our present consideration, though it ought not to be overlooked in judging of England's part in the general progress of the human race.

In like manner, and with an even greater degree of certainty, may we claim that so far as a race can be said to possess a common character, the English people possess a character whose formative influences have been even more varied, more manifold, and are much more clearly discernible, than those which combined to make them what they have recently proved themselves still to be, a race that cannot be surpassed for physical endurance.

If the salt of the sea is in their blood through their link with the old Vikings, many a social custom and many a religious rite testify that the dead faiths of pre-Christian ages are not as dead as they seem. The life of yesterday passes into the life of to-day, and no race, however long it may endure, can ever wholly free itself from its past. While, then, the voices of a past, so remote and untraceable, are still vocal, it would be strange, indeed, should we fail to hear with greater distinctness those which have spoken in more recent times.

When the voice of the Puritan was heard in our land, drowning others as truly English as his, it was not altogether well with us; but when his voice was for the time silenced, it went ill with us indeed, from which circumstance we may conclude that England thrives best with a tempered harmony, and that it would be unwise and impolitic to suppress any of the notes which may compose it.

To this remarkable admixture of natures and temperaments, so different and in some respects so conflicting, one of the most admirable qualities of the English may perhaps be attributed. There is nothing more characteristic of our island race than its spirit of compromise. To some ears the word has a disagreeable sound, but it serves our purpose well; and, indeed, there is nothing in it to cause shame, for compromise, as it is known amongst us, is generally as honourable as it is prudent and wise. If it has often saved a ministry from falling, it has as often mollified the anger of an opposition, promoted the well-being of the empire, and secured to us the blessing of peace. There can be little doubt that this spirit, which may well be described as a virtue, is the result of the working of many different political and religious forces upon each other, until each found in turn that it was impossible to have everything its own way, and that it could only be by means of a policy of give and take that the intellectual, moral and economic progress of the nation could be maintained.

There is no great law on the statute book of the realm which does not bear this characteristic

stamp. Motions, which upon their first introduction in Parliament aroused the fiercest opposition, and were denounced with a passionate
eloquence and an abundance of apparently un-
answerable argument, have in time found an
honourable place in our system of jurisprudence,
having, in their passage through the two houses,
undergone such change as made them not only
tolerable to both assemblies, but turned their
opponents into sponsors.

Again, the English Church, a knowledge of
which is so essential to the understanding of
England and the English people that one of our
shrewdest men of letters [1]—though not of that
Church himself—has pronounced it "more than
half the whole matter," is undoubtedly an institution which owes its present position to the
application of this same principle of compromise.
Its formularies, its ritual, its relation to the State,
its resemblance to and differences from every other
religious body in Christendom, all bear witness
to this fact, a fact which, if it makes its position
one of great strength in the nation, at the same
time exposes it to the ridicule of those who do not
or perhaps will not, understand it. "The Church
of England," writes one of this class, "has a
Catholic Prayer-Book, Calvinistic Articles and an
Arminian clergy." This, of course, if true, would
be the highest praise, and constitute one of the
Church's chief excellences. There is something
of real worth in each of the systems, Catholic,
Calvinistic, Arminian, and great indeed is the

---

[1] Thomas Carlyle.

Church that can embrace them all; in its comprehensiveness it would be admirably fitted to
be the spiritual home of a great and generous
people.

That all these differing elements, racial, tem-
peramental, religious, have, in the course of time,
been drawn together into one vast empire, with a
unity in diversity that is the admiration of our
friends and the despair of our enemies, is indeed
a noble achievement; nor could we now contemplate, without dismay, the possible elimination of
any one of them. England has become what it
is to-day through the contribution of each to the
growth of the national life. Selecting one of these
elements, we shall examine what it has done to
mould, through its influence on religious and
political thought, the character of the race, a race
(be it ever remembered) that has spread itself over
the whole earth and given laws and rulers to four
hundred millions of its inhabitants, besides the
preponderant part it has borne both in populating
the United States of America and in laying the
foundations of those political and religious insti-
tations which, more than anything else, have contributed to the building of these States into the
greatest Republic the world has ever seen.

Of all the movements which England has
experienced since the upheaval of the sixteenth
century, none has been more exposed than the
Puritan to the jibes of an unfriendly criticism.
It would seem deliberately and of set purpose to
have bared its back to the smiter. It has provided excellent copy for the novelist and the

B

historian, and the popular preacher has made fine play with its undoubted defects. The mannerisms and eccentricities, the affectations and hypocrisies of its professed followers, their roughness, their bigotry, their contempt of sacred places, have all been set out in their most objectionable features, and lashed with an unsparing severity; while even those who have honourably and truthfully defended the principles for which Puritanism stands, have failed to remove, from the public mind, the prejudices created by writers of a more popular type of literature. It is not that Puritanism has lacked able advocates; there are many works of the highest value, works entirely reliable, which have upheld its cause with conspicuous ability; but for one person who will read the Memoirs of Colonel Hutchinson, Baxter's "Self Review," or the admirable apologetics of Stoughton, a hundred will derive their knowledge from the fascinating pages of Woodstock. It is, of course, quite possible that the detractors of the movement have overshot the mark in often painting the typical Puritan as little better than a villainous hypocrite, forgetting that hypocrisy is the homage which vice pays to virtue, and that consequently the assumption of the garb and demeanour of the Puritan by a dissembler testified to the high character of the men of that persuasion. Be that as it may, Puritanism since the moment of its inception has had to encounter much opposition and misrepresentation. From the days of Barebones Parliament to the days of the despised Clapham Sect — when a bishop preferred that his carriage should draw up and its occupant alight in front of a tavern to alighting in front of the home of the saintly John Venn—the rulers of the earth have taken counsel against it.

It would be to little purpose to attempt either a denial or a justification of those glaring blemishes which made Puritanism unpopular from the beginning in the eyes of a large section of the English people, or furnished ground for the grave accusations which were laid against it, sometimes sorrowfully, more often with gleeful satisfaction. Almost all its faults, on the moral side, may be traced to one cause, the failure on the part of the most devout and upright of its teachers to recognise human nature ; they forgot or overlooked the fact that the best of men are but men at the best, and that if human beings "strive to wind themselves too high," sooner or later something must snap, something give way. In language somewhat overstrained, but in the main true, Mr. Coulton writes : " The pursuit of an exaggerated and impossible other-worldliness, with all its natural fruits of frequent formality and hypocrisy, has damaged for ever the reputation of that religious revival which for the first time found itself strong enough to force time-honoured ideas for a brief moment upon an unwilling nation."[1] It may be possible, and indeed ought to be possible, to make England a nation of honest, God-fearing folk, but it is beyond the bounds of possibility to make it a nation of saints, either of the Catholic or the Puritan type. It was in largest measure due to

---

[1] Coulton, " Medieval Studies," First Series, p. 45.

the ignoring of this apparently quite obvious fact
that Puritanism, in the decadent period immediately
preceding the Restoration, when it had lost the
first glow of its faith and began to fall back from
its high ideals, drew upon itself, not entirely without
justification, the pained lamentations of its friends
and the derision of its foes. Few would have
ventured at that period to prophecy for it a long
and glorious future, a future which would enable
it to stamp the impression of its religious and
political ideas on the whole Anglo-Saxon race,
colouring even that section of the English Church,
which at one time had been its bitterest opponent,
with the doctrinal views and devotional thought
of its foremost divines and writers, and winning
for many of them a high place in the affections
of religiously disposed men and women wherever
the English language is read.

Yet the explanation is easy. Beneath what was
merely outward and accidental in Puritanism,
beneath occasional lapses on the part of some of
the " professors "—scandalising " the Godly " and
discrediting the cause—there breathed the Hebrew
spirit of righteousness ; persistent and unquenchable, even where practice ill-accorded with principle.
Episcopacy was suppressed, Independency exalted,
Parliaments rudely dissolved. It seemed to be a
reign of tyranny, but there was method in all this
madness, and, if we take long views, beyond this
time of distress we shall see that the direction in
which Oliver set his face, when once he, and at
an earlier period Pym, struck for a free Parliament,
must at length lead to liberty of conscience, liberty

of worship, political liberty, enabling free men to make their own laws in a freely elected House of Commons; for even at the time when the hand of the Independents was heaviest, and Oliver's rule most rigorous, the vast majority of his army cherished hopes of political and religious peace and a return to their homes and civil life. " Their political ideals were few, but very definite, and held with intense tenacity: religious freedom, orderly government, and the final abolition of the abuses for which Laud and Charles had died."[1] Such principles as these, always dear to the English mind, though sometimes forgotten by their stoutest advocates, were at length recognised as the unshakable pillars on which the movement must rest, and which alone could ensure for it honour and length of days.

---

[1] Frederick Harrison, " Cromwell," p. 170.

CHAPTER II

SOME CAUSES CONTRIBUTORY TO THE GROWTH
OF PURITANISM

PURITANISM was no new thing, freshly sprung from the ground or sent down from heaven. " That which hath been is now, and that which is to be hath already been." The Novatians of the third century of Christianity, standing out for purity of doctrine and rectitude of conduct, as matters of vastly greater importance than Church rites and ceremonies, assumed a similar title; and, long before the Christian era, Eastern religions, including Judaism, furnished types of character, which sometimes in combination, sometimes alone, witnessed for principles not altogether unlike those of the English Sectaries of the seventeenth century. It must, however, be confessed that in such movements, and especially in that of the Novatians, the motives were not always of the highest nor the characters of the actors the best; yet these are blemishes incidental to, and perhaps inseparable from, every reform undertaken by man. There was, perhaps, charity of judgment as well as pathos in the comment of the Hebrew poet, who wrote, "To all perfection I have seen a limit." "Puritanism," says Lord Morley, " came from the deeps. It was a manifestation of elements in

human nature that are indestructible. It flowed
from yearnings that make themselves felt in
Eastern world and in Western; it sprang from
aspirations that breathe in men and women of
many faiths and communions."

This is quite true, and the important and sad
fact is that these aspirations, breathing in many
of the noblest natures in England—it is sufficient
to mention only such names as Pym, Milton,
Hutchinson—were not considered, nor was there
any serious attempt made to satisfy them on the
part of the National Church and the Court party.
Possibly James, for instance, like Elizabeth, could
not understand the Puritans. His mind was cast
in a different mould, and his vanity, always tempt-
ing him to display his learning where an opportunity offered, would not suffer him to admit that
such men as Pym had any case worth hearing.
" Your Majesty should hear the other side."
" The other side! One side is enough for an
honest man." As Pym and others approached
him with a petition at Newmarket, he maintained
his character as the "most learned fool in Christendom" by calling out, "Chairs, chairs, here be twal
kynges comin." When men of high position and
unblemished character are treated with derision
by one who, if Monarchy be rightly understood,
stands in the relation of a father to his subjects,
loyalty is strained. Yet singularly enough James
was sufficiently shrewd to recognise the unwisdom
of Laud's proceedings with the Scotch, which he
described as " an ill-fangled platform to make that
stubborn Kirk stoop more to the English platform.

He knows not the stomach of that people." But
the fooling of James was a small matter compared
with what the Puritans endured when Charles
and Laud and Strafford began their policy of
" thorough."

An ingenious lecturer has advanced the idea that
Michael Angelo was the originator of the Reformation. His magnificent work demanded a worthier
shrine than old St. Peter's. The Pope resolved
to have it re-built ; for this money was required,
and forth goes Tetzel with his indulgences, which
aroused the wrath of Luther and therefrom sprang
the Reformation. With much greater plausibility
might we argue that Puritanism, as a system
which overthrew the Monarchy and the Church,
set up Independency in the Army and Presbyterianism in the State, owed its origin to the King
and his ministers and his archbishop. Tactfully
handled, and with reasonable concessions, the
movement might have found a home in theNational
Church, but unfortunately tact and reasonableness
were qualities that had no place in the breasts of
this unhappy triumvirate. " This jumping upon
things at first dash will destroy all. To keep up
Friendship, there must be little addresses and
applications."[1]

They must have forgotten the fact that they
were dealing with Englishmen, with men of an
altogether unique character. " The Englishman
as a rule," says a modern writer, " has small love
for ideas, he does not think deeply or carefully
about abstract truth ; his interest lies in facts

---

[1] Selden, " Table Talk."

and in what he can make of them. He has a high
sense of duty, and he does his duty simply and
bravely without much consideration of why he
does it. In the second place he is insular. The
welfare of the nation means much to him and he
looks little beyond it. If he cares for the National
Church, it is as a national institution he cares for
it. In religion, as in other things, he likes to go
his own way and "muddle through." In the
third place he is extremely independent. He does
not drive and he refuses to be driven. Religion
and morality appear to him as personal rather
than corporate concerns, and he dislikes the claim
of the Church to exercise authority over him. He
cares for freedom of speech and action more than
he cares for the correspondence of either with
exact truth. He is very tolerant of all that does
not seriously outrage his conscience, and expects
from others the same tolerance that he is ready
to grant."[1]

In this very fair analysis of the English character we have an explanation of the Puritan revolt.
Folly surpassed itself in the handling of those
strong-willed, righteous, narrow-minded men of
the seventeenth century. If the matter were not
so serious we might say that some mischief-making
"Puck" had taken possession of the minds of
the King and his advisers, for certainly stupidity
and obstinacy are not sufficient to account for the
attitude they assumed towards half the nation,
towards men upright, honest, and by no means
ill-disposed towards Monarchy or to the Church as

---

[1] H. L. Goudge, "Duty of a National Church, " p. 41.

a national institution. That they were extremely
independent and unwilling to be driven, is only
to say that they were English ; yet the course on
which the King and the archbishop were bent
meant the forfeiture of their independence and an
humble submission to be driven along a road they
had no mind to travel. Some excuse may be found
for Charles on the ground that he was to all intents
and purposes a foreigner, having little in common
with the English mind and the English character.
" His incurable weakness was that he never shook
off the Machiavelian or Medicean ' Prince,' and
never understood the nature of Englishmen."[1] On
the other hand his devotion to his bright, charming wife, which was one of the redeeming points
of his conduct, brought him under an influence
the most unfortunate that can be conceived of for a
man in his position. When judging this hapless
King, therefore, it is but right to remember that
along with his own ungenial and unaccommodating
temper and his unpardonable duplicity, other
circumstances combined to work his ruin. The
stars in their courses seemed to fight against
Charles. As events developed the more extreme
of the Sectaries became convinced that " the thing
was from the Lord " ; and that their enemies did
what they did that heaven might deliver them into
the hands of the godly, and thus the troublers of
His Israel be cut off. There can be no doubt that
the oppressor's hand had much to do with the
dissemination of the principles he sought to suppress,
and that many men who looked with a measure

---

[1] F. Harrison, " Oliver Cromwell," p. 105.

of suspicion on the movement in its earlier stages, were found at last willing to die for it. Short of a wholesale extermination, which is rarely possible, there seems to be no way of getting rid of heretics or troublesome opponents, and so long as they are not a danger to the State the wisest policy is to let them alone. England's modern method is to turn enemies into friends by long-suffering and by judicious compromise, and this admirable policy is in large measure due to the working of the Puritan leaven in the body politic ; but long experience has taught us that the surest way to popularise a new religious or political craze is to mulct it in the Law Courts, denounce it from the pulpit, and bring a few of its prophets to the block. " There's another hundred pounds in cousin Mary's pocket," exclaimed a relative of Mrs. Humphry Ward, as she listened to a foolish tirade against that gifted woman's book, " Robert Elsmere," by a popular and not very discreet clergyman. The rulers in France and Spain and the Pope of Rome were prescient enough to see that no good would come from this policy of " thorough," but its authors were determined to apply it with all their power ; and great as the consequent sufferings and inconveniences of the Sectaries must have been, there is no room for doubt that the decision to root them out contributed as much as any other cause to rooting them firmly in. There is, perhaps, a natural tendency on the part of apologists like Stoughton to exaggerate the sufferings of the persecuted sects, and Professor Usher finds some support for his contention that the flight to Europe

and to America was not occasioned wholly by the
severity of their trials,[1] in the fact that many
staunch Puritan clergy remained in the Church and
continued to minister to appreciative congregations;
but when every allowance of this character is made,
the weight of evidence is too great, and the voice
of Milton too resounding to enable us to cast any
doubt on the fearful sufferings of " the just " at
that period. "I bear in my body the marks of
the Lord Jesus," was no vain boast on the part of
men who, in addition to the confiscation of property,
suffered tortures and mutilation of their bodies
for conscience sake.

Here then do we find one of the chief sources of
the growth and strength of Puritanism. Regarded
as a political and religious movement destined to
influence ages yet to come and races as yet hardly
in being, its worst enemies proved its best
friends. They that were scattered upon the
persecution of the Sectaries went everywhere
preaching the Word and propagating their political ideals.

The Tudor divines on the other hand, had held
and taught doctrines which were of the very essence
of the Puritan faith. In proof whereof it is sufficient to mention : " the right of every Christian
man to approach his Maker without the interven-
tion of a priest," that "no form of Church government is essential to the existence of a Church,"
though some may be better than others, " that

[1] " The Pilgrims and their History," by Ronald C. Usher.
But see Professor Macfaden's reply, *Spectator*, April 5th,
1919.

the Pope is anti-Christ,[1] and the Church of Rome
mystical Babylon." Even the learned author of
the Ecclesiastical Polity, Richard Hooker, the
hammer of the factious Puritan, declares that " so
far forth as the Church is the mystical body of
Christ and His invisible spouse, it needeth no
external polity." It is conceivable that if Cranmer's scheme of uniting all the Reformed Churches
into one great Protestant federation had materialised, and if Charles and Laud and Wentworth had
never existed, the Puritan revolt would never have
taken place. But this would not have prevented
the growth of Puritan religious doctrines and
political principles, it would the rather have provided an easier path for their progress.

Again, the Puritan was a man of one book, and
that book the English Bible. He regarded the
Scriptures as a final authority on all subjects,
national and ecclesiastical. All the books in the
sacred volume were of equal value, and every word
inspired. At great length it was expounded in
the pulpit. It was read in the home, its most con-
solatory passages memorised, its terrible denun-
ciations, in their most literal sense, applied to the
ungodly ; and so deeply did this mingled awe and
love of the holy Book penetrate the national life,
that to this day, after all that criticism, higher and
lower, has done for us, Chillingworth's assertion
remains true, " the Bible and the Bible alone is
the religion of Protestants." It is true, that not
all the Puritans shared these extreme views, though
none of them lacked the profoundest reverence

---

[1] High Churchmen, like George Herbert, held this view.

for the Book. Baxter for instance, was content
to say that it was enough for him that the Gospels
were the work of godly, honest men, who had
knowledge of the things they wrote of. It will,
however, be readily understood that when men
read in an infallible Book, which was to them the
very Voice of the Eternal, that Kings were the
chosen of the nation as well as the anointed of the
Lord, that even David did not sit on the throne
before an united nation set him on it, that in the
Kingdom of God there is no respect of persons, all
the elect being equal, that even Apostles dis-
claimed lordship over God's heritage ; the divine
right of Kings, passive obedience, and the exclusive
rule of bishops, were claims which all rested on a
very shaky foundation, and if pressed to extremes
must inevitably fall. These claims, in a modified
form might have been tolerated, but tolerated only
on a frank admission that they were not essential
to the life of Church or State. Puritanism from
its first breath meant a democracy, or a constitutional Monarchy, so limited as to be in practice a
democracy.

The matter in dispute between the two parties
into which the country came to be divided, is fully
if tersely expressed in the protestation of Lords
and Commons made on May 26th, 1642 : " This
erroneous maxim (the absolute supremacy of the
King) being infused into Princes that their Kingdoms are their own and that they may do what
they will, as if their kingdoms were for them, and
not they for their kingdoms ! " [1] Here are two

---

[1] " Social England," vol. IV.

absolutely hostile principles which unhappily admitted no compromise, so that the matter must be fought out to the bitter end. So complete has been the triumph of the Puritan conception of Sovereignty, overbearing all opponents, that in every state or dominion where the Anglo-Saxon language is spoken the will of the people is now supreme. Indeed, it is not a little remarkable that in the British Empire with its Monarchy, this principle acts with a greater degree of freedom than in America, with a Republic.

CHAPTER III

BOTH friend and enemy bore a part as already noted, in making a permanent habitation in England for the religious and political ideals of the Parliamentary party; the one of set purpose, the other unconsciously. The King, the bishops, the House of Lords and Strafford, were the unconscious instruments; John Pym, than whom England has had few greater commoners, the conscious and deliberate instrument. We have seen the Upper House shorn of all but a semblance of authority over the doings of the Commons by the Parliament Act of 1911, but historical students will recognize that both that Act and the Reform Bill of 1832, were in truth the measures of Pym fully as much as the measures of their immediate promoters. When Pym, in the days of the Long Parliament, warned the Lords that failure on their part to act in concert with the Lower House "would only force theCommons to save the kingdom alone," he spoke the language of the twentieth century English politician, and set in motion forces which culminated in changing an absolute Monarchy and a subordinate Parliament into what is now practically a Republic with an hereditary Prince as its head. If England is to-day in possession of

20

the best constitution the wit of man can devise—
an Upper House as a revising and advisory chamber,
a constitutional Monarch, with enhanced moral
influence, and an untrammelled Commons—to
Pym and the Puritan leaders in the Long Parliament we owe this inheritance. If, again, we have an
Established Church in close connection with the
State, possessing large liberty itself but having
no power, and in our day no inclination, to withhold
it from other communions, that also is the fruit
of their labours. Baxter tells of a shrewd Independent neighbour who remarked to him that he
thanked God they had held power long enough
to fix their principles in England for ever. The
Restoration came too late to undo the work of fifty
years, for we may think of the leaven of Puritanism
working in the hearts of the people at least from
the early days of the first James.

Had the characters and abilities of such leaders
as Eliot, Hampden, and Pym been hereditary, the
corruptions which still attach to our political life,
and have indeed become more acute in recent
years, would most certainly have been abolished
long ago, or reduced to the smallest proportions.
The King, with a small advisory Committee elected
by both Houses would be the sole fountain of
honour, and dignities and titles no longer sold
for replenishing the coffers of political parties ;
for it cannot be asserted too often or too strongly
that the nobler spirits in the Parliament, and later
in the army, were all for a constitutional Monarch,
while some of them were filled with a passionate
loyalty to the throne. Time has given us a

c

constitutional Monarchy, but not another Pym. The fact just mentioned is easily recognised in the attitude of a large body of the strongest advocates of a free Parliament towards the King, when matters reached a climax. They were in favour of a more humane course than that which was taken, being by no means ill-disposed towards Charles personally, partly through a sentiment of loyalty, and partly through a preference for Monarchy to any other form of rule. And in the earlier stages of the war between King and Parliament, we know that Baxter and many of his clerical brethren "in the simplicity of their hearts," believed that Essex, Waller and Cromwell were really fighting the battles of Charles, "and that their real object was to rescue the King from the thraldom of the malignants, and the Church from the tyranny of the Prelatists."[1]

"We kept," says Baxter, "to our old principles, and thought others had done so too, except a few inconsiderable persons," and although afterwards in his controversial works he vindicates the war on Charles, he does not do so as an enemy of Monarchy but as a friend of freedom.

But to return to Pym, it should be borne in mind that all the circumstances were favourable to enabling him to make a deep and lasting impression on the country. The bold and patriotic action of Eliot in his impeachment of Buckingham, the courage and fortitude of Hampden in resisting the payment of ship money, imposed without the sanction of Parlia-

---

[1] Sir J. Stephen's Essay on Baxter, p. 78.

ment, and the heartless treatment meted
out to Eliot, who lay in the Tower to his death,
were still fresh in men's minds. It would hardly
have been possible to select, in the England of
those days, two men of higher character and of
purer and more disinterested motives ; and it was
on these the resentment of the King fell, in one case
harmlessly, in the other fatally. Englishmen, even
when their own lives are far from exemplary, are
always affected by purity in men of high position ;
they are proud of royalty when the Court is above
reproach ; and when they happen upon a politician
who wins their confidence in an exceptional degree,
so strong is this feeling, they will often endow him
in their minds with virtues which he may only
possess in very limited measure. Here, at all
events, the esteem was well founded, and it was
with the memory of what Eliot and Hampden had
dared for their country deep in the hearts of the
people, that Pym took up his parable in the Parliament of 1640. From the first moment his course
lay clear before him, and he resolved at any cost,
at any sacrifice, to follow it. He was now practically the sole leader of the party that stood for
liberty and law. Edward Coke, the eminent
lawyer, who was largely responsible for the Petition
of Right, was dead, " Eliot had perished in the
Tower ; Cotton's heart was broken," Oliver St.
John, a shrewd observer, took little part in leadership, and Wentworth had apostatised. These
circumstances lend all the more grandeur to the
solitary figure of the great Englishman who felt
his country's needs, recognised that its foes were

those of its own house, and through the gathering storm saw with sure and steady gaze the rising of the sun of freedom and peace.

Almost all the prominent men of the party were of gentle birth and good education. They belonged, for the most part, to the country gentleman class, a class much attached to English institutions, infected with no revolutionary tendencies, and deeply imbued with a love of English liberty. It must have been a source of strength to men of this class, and a great encouragement to them, that the first man of letters in the country, who for all time Englishmen will reckon as second only to Shakespeare, John Milton, was actively. on their side. It is true Johnson makes light of his services to the cause, and gives anything but a pleasing impression of the great poet, at the time he was instructing his undistinguished group of pupils at his "private academy" in Aldersgate Street. Johnson would perhaps have had him writing ballads on liberty while earning his bread as a pedagogue, but Milton's pen was not idle, nor his influence inconsiderable, from the hour of his return from the continent to his native country. It is indeed to be feared that the eminent biographer was not himself altogether free from the peevishness he attributes to Milton, for if the latter bears hard on the prelates in some of his tracts, the Royalist party and the English Church have had few more prejudiced apologists than Johnson; it would, however, hardly have been seemly if this robust and transparently honest Tory had allowed Milton

to escape scot-free, and we dismiss his opinion
with the lenient comment of a later scribe that it
is "a remarkable instance of insuperable antipathy striving to be fair."

What we are here concerned with, however,
is the part Milton played in supporting the claims
of the Parliament, and the influence his works
have had on later generations in moulding thought
and fostering the love of liberty. The readers
of "Lycidas" and "Areopagitica" were probably
few, and it is hardly possible that even his political tracts reached a large multitude, in days
when few peasants could read; but the few who
assimilated his ideas were able to pass them on
to others, and so it has come to pass that many
who have never handled a volume of Milton or
heard his name, have yet become indoctrinated
with the principles he taught. The country has
not followed him in his unreasonable hatred of
prelacy and Monarchy, in his sympathy with
Republicanism, in the Arian views he adopted in
his later years or his anti-Sabbatarianism and his
loose views on marriage. To the modern Puritan
all these make matter for regret; but as a champion of the rights of the people, and of freedom
of speech and of the Press he will never be forgotten, while students of English literature will
always assign him a place amongst the immortals.

It is not necessary, in a sketch that aims at
exhibiting tendencies and permanent influences,
to call up every character that played a part in
bringing these to a head, but it would be impossible in dealing with the political tendencies

of those times to overlook the most prominent
figure of all, that of the Protector. Cromwell
was not the able politician we see in Pym. He
was of the cut-and-thrust pattern when dealing
with refractory Englishmen, though a diplo-
matist of surpassing ability when dealing with
foreign chancelleries.[1] We are chiefly interested
in him, and the men who stood nearest to him in
spiritual outlook, as the prime movers in the
revolution, and the upholders of Independency
in preference to Presbyterianism. It is important
to bear in mind that neither the revolution
nor Independency was necessary to Puritanism.
The principles of the movement, both political
and religious, could, under favouring circumstances, have taken root and flourished in the
National Church; and, indeed, succeeded in
doing so, sporadically at first, and afterwards in
larger measure. Besides, we are at liberty to
assume, without offence, that Independency as
a church polity has not in it the element of permanency, and as for the revolution it is matter of
history that its life was as short as it was stormy.
It came and went with Oliver. We need not
examine the causes of its downfall, for we know
that its position was from the first precarious.
Cromwell and the Army, fairly judged, were
tolerant, and heartily desired religious liberty.
The Presbyterian party, unlike their brethren of
to-day, held views on Church government that

---

[1] Macaulay ("Hist. England," Vol. I.) regards him in this
respect the "profoundest politician in Europe." Here we
are considering his ability to manage Parliament.

equalled, if they did not outrival, those of the papacy; while several small fanatical sects kept the whole Puritan movement in a constant state of ferment. In the circumstances force was necessary in order that Cromwell might hold his own. Here were difficulties and troubles of no ordinary kind, for if we recall the real principles of the Puritans, advocated by such men as Pym— liberty of conscience, freedom of Parliament— we see at once the absurdity of the position. The ideals of Puritanism could not be promoted by force, and Cromwell, unwillingly, we may believe, was obliged to rely on force.[1] It is one thing to overthrow a Monarchy, quite another to establish a new sort of kingdom whose foundations are liberty and peace, but which is kept in position by the sword. Such an incongruity could not last. It is no wonder therefore that the really effective revolution came later, and had no more part in Cromwell than if he had never been born; for this later revolution " was aristocratic and not democratic, secular not religious, parliamentary and not military, the substitution for the old monarchy of a territorial oligarchy, supreme alike in Lords and Commons."[2] And then followed the long reign of squire and parson, over the length and breadth of rural England; and surely nothing could have been more contrary

---

[1] That "the honest party" owed its pre-eminence to the sword was to him an unfortunate accident, which he strove to mitigate, but which, in the nature of things, it was impossible for him to shake off.—Gardiner, " History of Commonwealth," Vol. III.

[2] Morley's " Cromwell."

to Oliver's mind, or more harmful to his projects. But if for a time the political revolution failed, a greater force remained. "It is in Milton and Bunyan," writes Morley, "rather than in Cromwell that we seek what was deepest, loftiest, and most abiding in Puritanism. We look to its apostles rather than its soldier."[1]

Yet this was by no means the end of Puritan political ideals. Like a stream running underground they remained partially hidden through the long period from the Restoration to the Victorian era, when they found an opening, created by the Act of 1832, and sprang up again like a fountain. Democracy, in its modern tendencies, would probably have found little favour had it appeared in Oliver's day, but it is as truly the offspring of the political tendencies of those times, as the Free Churches in modern England are the offspring of Puritan religious ideals. The brook became a river and the river a sea.

In what has been here written of Pym, it will be seen that there is anything but acquiescence in the opinion held by Carlyle, who describes his speeches as "barren as brick clay," and still less in that of Wade, whose singularly unsympathetic summing up of Pym's character is surprising in one who went to the trouble of writing his life. If Pym had been the subtle plotter Wade would have us believe, yet a man of no foresight, no definite policy, no vision or initiative, possessed of power to destroy, but with no ability to erect, it is a wonder he thought it worth while to honour

---

[1] Morley's "Cromwell."

him with so much attention. It is hoped that the estimate formed of him in these pages is juster and truer to fact. It is evident that he aimed at three things, a constitutional Monarch, a freely elected Parliament and the supremacy of the House of Commons. That all three did not come in his time was due to circumstances beyond his control, and that they came by a more circuitous and stormy route than he would have wished, was in no sense due to mismanagement on his part. The point to keep in view is that all of them are in our possession now, just as Pym would have desired. His policy, to the extent indicated here, has triumphed and his principles to a similar extent, are now a part of the British constitution.

CHAPTER IV

THE RELIGIOUS TENDENCIES OF PURITANISM

IT is no part of the task of an essayist who is looking chiefly at final results, to record, minutely, events and the characters of the actors who took part in them, after the manner of an historian; and for that reason the more unpleasant aspects of Puritanism, which we may charitably regard as being of the nature of the birth-throes of the movement, need not occupy our attention at any great length. Fanaticism, bigotry, intolerance, unreasonableness, strife, jealousies, are all there, and it would be a thankless and futile undertaking either to attempt to explain them away or to excuse them. That the fanatics, who formed a considerable section of the party were regicides, and never repented of the deed, that Milton wrote in justification of it, that Cromwell burst out into coarse horse-play—perhaps to conceal a more tender feeling—upon signing the deed of execution, are well attested facts of history. On this, the the darkest deed of the party, however, something must be said in passing.

Cromwell, according to some popular historians, ruined both his cause and his reputation by the execution of Charles, an act which they condemn in unmeasured terms, and which few, indeed, can be found to support. But it would be more to the point if they had suggested a workable alternative. The members who remained in Parliament after Pride's purge, must have found themselves in an embarrassing position with an uncrowned King on their hands, who was not amenable to reason, and whose views of his kingly prerogatives justified to his own conscience a course of prevarication, evasion, and faithlessness to his most solemn pledges; a course which was all the more dangerous to the liberty of his subjects because it was conscientious. The execution may have been a blunder, and had very little of the quality of mercy to relieve it; but to leave him at large or imprison him for life were courses equally out of the question; and the circumstances hardly admitted the application of the aphorism of a witty Puritan preacher, " of two evils choose neither." It should, however, be remembered to their undying credit that, not long before the King's pathetic end, Cromwell and Ireton had risked their lives in a vain effort to bring him to reason.

There it seems we must leave the matter; but it is doubtful if any modern Puritan could without emotion stand to-day on Chester Wall, and read, for the first time, the inscription which tells that at that spot Charles stood and saw the defeat of his troops by the Parliamentary Army. Feeling is gentler, judgments more charitable, than in those rough, strenuous times. But, if the spectator be just, he will at the same time admit that such was the price England had to

pay for its liberties. As regards the more tragic
event, many will say the same, though opinion
will always be divided on the subject.

If we now turn to things of a more agreeable
character, we shall find them in abundance.
Cromwell began life as a member of the Church
of England, wherein he was baptized and in which
he worshipped, when residing quietly at his home
in Huntingdonshire. He became an Independent,
and ended as an uncompromising advocate of
religious toleration. At the time when popular
feeling was against the Jews, he was favourable
to their residence in England ; and, as evidence
of the perpetuation of his views, to this day the
English Puritan takes the warmest interest in
their spiritual and temporal welfare, generously
supporting societies whose object is their conversion to Christianity, and, like Cromwell, urging
in and out of season their right to the land of
Palestine and the restoration of their national
life. "It was the Puritan love of the Bible,"
writes Sokolow, in his recently published "History
of Zionism," "dominating the whole domestic and
political life of the English people for some centuries, predisposed them to be favourable to the
Jews." In the later period of the Protectorate,
Cromwell went much further than this by extending toleration to unorthodox Sectaries, such as
the Socinians, and even assuring Mazarin that he
would go as far as was reasonable in conceding toleration to Roman Catholics. "I had far
rather tolerate Mohammedanism," said Oliver
on one occasion " than that one of God's children

should suffer." It must, however, be admitted that the promised liberty never came ; one of the last acts of the Cromwellian Parliament being directed against the " Papists " ; nor did Episcopacy ever win the goodwill of the Independents, for from the comprehensive Church, which Cromwell proposed, but never established, Episcopalians were explicitly excluded. But the liberalising tendency had taken root and was bound to grow in future years. It is an easy matter for detractors of Oliver and his co-religionists to point to instances of exceptional harshness and intolerance, they are numerous enough, but this is to overlook the fact that the principle of toleration having once been acknowledged and accepted, nothing could hinder its development, until it has become one of England's most precious inheritances ; though it is unfortunately true the principle has often been widely departed from. A more doubtful proposition is that advanced by Morley, that not to Puritanism but to Rationalism is due the credit of liberalising all our English institutions. This assertion would need for its support the inadmissible assumptions that the men of the seventeenth century, who struggled for freedom in Parliament and the field, were Rationalists, and that the spirit of Rationalism has dominated English politics and English religious opinion from the seventeenth century to the present time. To state the case thus is to expose its absurdity. Again, the exceptional treatment of Roman Catholics, about which Macaulay and Green make much ado, can be justified to some extent ; for the Roman Church, conceding nothing and demanding much, must ever prove a difficulty to the liberal reformer. "You cannot," says Froude, "tolerate what will not tolerate you, and is trying to cut your throat."

It would hardly be an exaggeration if we should suggest that the publication of Oliver's Proclamation of 1655, granting religious liberty, without apparently any qualifying clauses, laid the foundation of that freedom of worship which we now enjoy. It was a proclamation so entirely after the mind of the English people that it has become a rooted principle among us, and we should find it hard to think there was ever a time when any other existed. The rebuke which Cromwell administered to Crawford, when the latter objected to a capable and trustworthy man on account of his religion, "the State in choosing men to serve it, takes no notice of their opinions," expresses the general view of the modern English mind, and at the same time proves that the Protector's policy of toleration was not prompted by mere expediency. But along with the grant of freedom of worship, contained in the Proclamation, sharp, threatening language is used against any who might presume to interfere with the liberties of others ; and it will appear strange to those who only know Quakerism through its modern professors, that those threats were directed in a special measure against George Fox and his followers. Gentleness, reasonableness, tender benevolence, are the virtues suggested to our minds by the

very mention of the name Quaker; and we should
be astonished beyond measure to hear of any man
of that persuasion, to-day, railing at magistrates,
refusing to remove his hat in Church, calling out
to a popular preacher, "Come down, you dog!
'Come down, you hireling,' or 'testifying to the
truth' by stripping himself naked and walking
up and down Smithfield.[1] Yet such are the
charges history records against them, and, so far
as they are true, we can only say in the first place
that the Protector's leniency in dealing with them
deserves our admiration, and in the second, that
the modern Quaker is a great improvement on
his ancestors.

When we pay regard not only to the acts of the
Protector but to the general trend of his views,
and those of the Army, towards an ever-increasing
toleration, and contrast the Puritan attitude at
its best with the sentiments and policy of Laud
and the Court party, we can judge at once which
of the two has had the greater influence upon the
mind of the country.

As regards the relation of the Church to the
State, the Independents were wholly in favour of
a close connection between them, Milton alone,
among the leading spirits of the age, being in
favour of their separation. Cromwell could not
conceive of the divorce of religion from politics,
sharing Pym's views on this subject, and holding
that a Christian must be a politician as much as
a preacher of righteousness. That man is recreant
to the ideals of Christianity who does not exercise

---

[1] Gardiner, "History of the Commonwealth," Vol. III.

himself to secure just laws for the State, as well as purity of doctrine in the Church. " If any whosoever," says Cromwell, "think the interests of Christians and the interests of the nation inconsistent, or two different things, I wish my soul may never enter into their secret." Obviously the Protector was no Liberationist, and that his opinion is again reviving amongst English middle-class politicians, is seen in the regret, that is now freely expressed, at the disendowment of the Welsh Church, and in the decline of interest in the Liberationist Society. The English Church might be sure of its position for a long time, if not for all time, could the clergy be persuaded to obey the law and to refrain from fussy interference with its present relation to the State, which certainly is not grievous. On the other hand, Cromwell's idea of a comprehensive Church, but on much more generous principles, embracing the whole of Anglo-Saxon Christianity, has become one of the most popular conceptions of our times, and is daily gaining ground.

The Synod of Dort, held in 1619, is supposed to have been the occasion of the ossifying of Calvinistic tenets, which from that date became characteristic of early Puritanism. But even Calvinism did not produce an absolutely uniform system of doctrine ; the Calvinists amongst Churchmen holding that Christ died for all, but that only the elect would be saved, while the strict Independents maintained that He died only for the elect. It is entirely contrary to fact that Arminianism was, as Morley seems to think,[1] crushed by the decisions of this Synod, for we find Cromwell, not many years later, pleading for liberty of conscience on behalf of some Arminians in his army; and, what is much more to the point, in considering the development of the movement, the Puritan of our time is either mildly Calvinistic or, as is more frequently the case, decidedly Arminian. If philosophy is as some believe, tending more and more in the direction of freedom as against determinism, it must undermine some of the foundations of the Calvinistic system of belief, so that it would be no longer necessary for a man to be a Calvinist in order to make good his claim to be in the Puritan succession. At the same time the great outstanding doctrines of the Divine Sovereignty and the Divine Omnipotence, the rock on which Calvin built his system, continue to hold their position; although it is possible that the doctrine of human free-will must impose on all who hold it, the necessity of postulating something like a voluntary limiting of omnipotence on the part of the Creator. Such considerations as these, though more or less by the way, far from cutting off the Puritan of our time from the men of the Commonwealth, really bear witness to the persistent working of the principles for which Puritan theologians like Baxter, and mystics like Cromwell, contended. Liberate thought, grant the principle of the authority of conscience, and it is impossible to say "thus far shalt thou go and no further." We are witnesses of a similar development in the

---

[1] Morley's "Cromwell," pp. 11, 52, 56.

D

domain of politics. Has not the Tory of modern
times adopted, with honest conviction, some
positions which would have shocked even the Whig
party in the reign of William and Mary ? Yet he
would maintain his right to be regarded as the
representative of the party which stood for King
and Church in the Stuart period, and stands for
King and Church to-day. In saying so much we
do not, of course, forget that King and Church and
party, moving with the times, are so changed as
to bear little resemblance to their forbears in the
days of great Elizabeth or Charles. " The thing
which never changes dies," said Dean Stanley,
the institution which writes over its portals *semper
eadem* writes its own doom ; and Puritanism lives
in this twentieth century, a great force for righteousness, not because in thought and speech and garb
it resembles or is a replica of the Puritanism of
three hundred years ago, but because it has out-
grown all these, and adapted itself to the modes
and requirements of a new age. Yet there are
things it can never outgrow. The modern Puritan,
like the scribe instructed unto the Kingdom of
Heaven, brings forth from his treasury old things
as well as new. He reads the " Pilgrim's Progress "
and the " Saint's Everlasting Rest." There is
hardly a pious cottager from the Dart to the
Tweed, from the Severn to the Thames, on whose
shelf you will not see the matchless allegory of
the Bedford Tinker, side by side with the English
Bible, and often with them a volume of the greatest
Puritan preacher England ever produced, Charles
Haddon Spurgeon ; and possibly a copy of Wesley's

hymn-book. Baxter still finds a place in homes
of a higher class, not infrequently in friendly com-
panionship with Jeremy Taylor's "Holy Living
and Holy Dying," a happy instance of the growth
of the tolerant principles Oliver set in motion. So
long as devout Englishmen and English women
nourish their souls with works of this character,
Puritanism will continue to hallow and sweeten
domestic life, and to exercise a wholesome influence
upon our national and municipal politics. For
nothing is more certain than that the character
shaped in secret will stamp itself on all the public
acts of a man's life. Ruskin was something of a
literary vagrant, uttering reckless things in a
fascinating way, yet more often an illuminating
teacher. What could be more true than his contention that the characters of the great Italian
painters can be read in their masterpieces, and his
general conclusion therefrom that what we are
will always appear in what we do ? So far as the
English love truth, hate lies, keep faith, detest
shams, countenance honesty, they walk where
Hampden and Pym and Baxter walked ; their
character is true to the Puritan type at its best.
No one will maintain that to Puritanism alone
such excellences are due, but justice requires that
it be credited with a large share in producing
them. What matters most is that the years have
not worn them threadbare. In good measure,
though not to the extent we could wish, England
retains them still ; and men know it.

Not long since, three Englishmen penetrated a
part of the Western Sudan, where no European

had ever been seen. The natives looked askance and threatening, whereupon the interpreter advanced and spoke a few words. Instantly their countenances changed ; they hoisted the baggage on their shoulders, and went forward cheerfully and confident. " What did you say ? " inquired the leading member of the party. " I said you were English."

CHAPTER V

THE GROWTH OF PURITANISM IN CHURCH
AND STATE

" PURITANISM, that word of many shades." If
we were to attempt a survey of Puritanism in this
twentieth century, inquiring how far it has extended and whence it came, we should be compelled to revise the judgments of many of our
ablest scribes and historians. We could not,
without qualification, accept the opinion which
Morley seems to favour, that as a religious influence
it may be dated from the Synod of Dort, and that
of others that as a Political force it is to be reckoned
from the trial of Hampden. We should find it
more difficult still to agree with Overton that the
Evangelicals of the eighteenth century must be
carefully distinguished from the Puritan party,
or with Macaulay and Green when they make too
sharp a distinction between Puritanism and Presbyterianism. In their political aims these two
differed ; in doctrine they were practically agreed.
As a matter of fact, Puritanism in our day, as a
strong force both in politics and religion, draws its
life from all these, and, indeed, many other sources.
The differences amongst the many parties in the
Army and the Parliament and the Kirk, in the days

of the Commonwealth and the Protectorate, when the Puritan party had become a menagerie, a chaos rather than a cosmos, must not blind us to this fact. Certain hitherto unpublished letters, which are now available, in one of which Monk rails at Vane and Lambert, in another where a thorough-going Puritan reviles Cromwell for his high-handed proceedings, in language which would do justice to the most bigoted Royalist, in another which charges the Scotch with faithlessness to the Covenant and plots to bring back the King if only he will make the Kirk dominant ; such documents, while revealing nothing new, show the extent of the schisms in the body, and the heats of blind passion which swayed it now in one direction, now in another ; and they no doubt provide fresh material to anyone who has a mind to discredit the whole movement as a thing quite absurd and impossible. But the mind that is set on seeking chiefly for the full ripe fruits of Puritanism may well decline to be influenced by the vicissitudes of its wayward youth. It matters little to us now, except in the way of an object-lesson, that the rule of the saints was a political disaster, or that Cromwell, sorely against his will, had often to resort to methods which he condemned in Charles and Strafford.

These are things of the past, interesting as facts of history, but in no way of the essence of the movement or even helpful to its growth. The same may be said of such forms of Church government as Voluntaryism, or doctrines like Calvinism, or political parties, " Petitioners " and "Abhorrers," at all events in their more developed state as Whigs and Tories.

The ancestry of Puritanism, where it came from, what it stands for, to what extent it is an influence in the political and religious life of to-day ? ---these are the questions which must engage us, and, indeed, are the only questions which are of practical import to modern students. In following out such inquiries, matters of detail, in some way related to them, will of course present themselves for consideration from time to time, and cannot be ignored.

As regards the ancestry of the movement, on which something has already been said, the importance of Presbyterianism calls for attention ; for Presbyterianism is become one of the greatest moral and intellectual forces in the Christian Church of modern times. It must be granted that in the days of the Commonwealth it was by no means a thing of beauty, and by its selfishness and bigotry and underhand dealings came near to wrecking the designs of the lovers of liberty. Nevertheless, we believe those historians are at fault who have been at pains to prove that Presbyterianism and Puritanism are distinct from each other. This mistake has been occasioned, and naturally enough, by the very pronounced opposition of the Parliament, which had become strongly, though not wholly, Presbyterian, to the Army, which was as strongly Independent. It is well-known that, before Cromwell's dramatic expulsion of the Rump, Parliament had carried on negotiations with Charles which, if successful, would have destroyed all that the Army had fought for, and, in the end, Parliament itself; nevertheless, as subsequent events have proved, Presbyterianism as truly as Independency was tending all the time to some form of democratic rule in Church and State. As early as 1581 "The Second Book of Discipline," ratified by the General Assembly of the Church of Scotland, practically established Puritanism as doctrinally the religion of Scotland. When we come to examine later developments of the movement we shall find similar resemblances to the original type, with, of course, such modifications and differences as have been created by new circumstances. But we may safely lay it down as a rule that wherever we can trace the democratic spirit in the State—the principle that the will of the people must prevail—and the prominence of the lay element in the Church— there you have Puritanism, under whatever new or old name it may be pleased to designate itself, or strange fellowship it may have found.

If this contention holds good, it follows necessarily that, so far from Puritanism being a spent force, it has won all along the line ; for never were those principles in a stronger position than they occupy to-day. Carried to excess, as in Milton's case, they might lead to the denial of all authority, but under the restraint of the Conservative instinct, which is strong in the English people, they may be regarded as the best safeguards of liberty, political and religious. At all events, they are come to stay ; wise men will therefore make the best they can of them.

All the denominations, then, which make up English Christianity to-day have made contribution to this result, for in all the Puritan spirit has found a home ; and it is the spirit rather than the denomination that declares the character. In Churchman, Presbyterian, Independent, Baptist, and Quaker, however much they differed among themselves, the Puritan character existed and continues to exist. The National Church cannot deny that from the rise of the movement it had its sympathisers and followers in the Church. Pym and Cromwell were bred in the Church ; and Pym, as we have seen, had no quarrel either with Monarchy or a State Church; and that many others shared his views on these high matters is clearly seen in the firm attachment, under many trials, of a large section of Puritans to both. It was only when he began to discern something of the nature of a conspiracy, on the part of throne and altar, against the liberties of the people that he felt obliged to set himself in opposition to these institutions.

How often has history recorded the defeat of a great cause, even its apparent destruction, only to bear witness hereafter to its revival and triumph. The greatest Faith the world has known passed, more than once, through such an ordeal, and may have to pass through it again. Nothing affords stronger assurance of the existence of a righteous spirit governing the affairs of men than the persistence of truth. Suppressed to-day, it appears with renewed life to-morrow. Driven from its first stronghold, it finds another and a safer. The

troublesome reformer, who disturbs a peace of
selfishness and gross self-indulgence, is imprisoned,
banished or beheaded, and the tyrant flatters
himself he is secure. But the words which the
dead had uttered live in the memories of thousands,
and the cause for which he suffered is not dead ; it
only sleeps, to awake one day and shake a nation.

It has been taken for granted that Puritanism
had a short life. As soon as it was born it began
to stray, and the Merry Monarch and his courtesans,
and his corrupt and immoral Court, made quite an
end of it. " England, after a short fit of hysterical
piety, went to the dogs." Very true, alas ! too
true ; but it was never true as a whole ; nor did
England stay there ; neither was it true at any
moment that Puritanism utterly failed. No doubt
the love of many waxed cold, and this had come
about had the Restoration never taken place.
When youths were put in the stocks or fined for
walking through the green fields on the Sabbath,[1]
when honest men were deemed unfit for the
magistracy because they refused to outrage their
conscience by professing a whole-hearted agree-
ment with " the godly " which they did not feel,
we need not be surprised that the " poor worn "
man began to feel the burden more than he could
bear, and that in the homes of many who " did
run well " Butler's " Hudibras " displaced the
" Saint's Rest," and many a professor left the
narrow way. Yet these facts do not justify us in
speaking of the decline or decay of Puritanism.
The Ten Commandments are a good rule of life,

---

[1] Gardiner, " History of Commonwealth," Vol. III.

but the conventionalities of religion or of society are no necessary part of them; and it was in reality the absurd conventionalities of the movement that were upon trial, and suffered the slings and arrows of outrageous fortune under the Stuarts, much more than the essential principles of Puritanism.

Truth compels the admission that very much in the manner in which some early Christians courted martyrdom, many of the extreme Sectaries were at great pains to make themselves disagreeable. When we read of the audience Charles II. granted Fox, his patience and amused interest in listening to his views—though the interview may recall that of Herod and John Baptist—we can hardly doubt that if the temper of the Sectaries had been more accommodating their lot would have been easier.

But through all those dark times, when the morals of the nation were being corrupted by the example in high places, the wealth of the country wasting away, its honour and its political influence rapidly declining, Puritanism, which had disappeared from the Court, though not from the Parliament, was silently growing, like seed rooting itself underground, to manifest itself in happier days and in wiser methods, purged of its excrescences, as a great moral and political power amongst the inhabitants of the British Islands and their brethren overseas.

Parliament, even in the reign of Charles the Second, had no lack of just and far-seeing men. Ashley, though of no decided faith, upheld

Protestantism and toleration on political grounds; the Country party, led by the heads of great families like the Russells, and Cavendishes, was favourable to the Whig and Protestant interests, and after the disgraceful Dover plot, by means of which Holland was to be destroyed and the Roman Church set up again in England, came to light, the Protestant cause gathered great strength. Other events worked in a similar way to promote it. The common people had not forgotten the faith and courage with which men like Harrison met death after the Restoration, the disinterring of the remains of the Protector and many of his party, and the outrages offered to them, outrages as contemptible as they were senseless. All these things sank deep into the public mind, and helped to make the Puritan future as safe outside, as the nobler spirits in the Commons kept it safe inside Parliament.

Thus we see that at a time when Puritanism, to all appearances, had lost power, and had no voice in the places made sacred to the party by Oliver's devout exercises and Scriptural quotations; when it was mocked by the rabble in the streets and held up to contempt in many a church pulpit, it was in reality growing in strength, through a remarkable confluence of circumstances, which may, without affectation, be described as providential.

CHAPTER VI

GROWING POWER OF THE HOUSE OF COMMONS

WE have seen that all through the reigns of James and Charles the First, King and Parliament contested for the mastery. Were the people's representatives to control taxation and expenditure? Was the Executive the servant of the King or was it to be directly responsible to the elected House? These were the burning questions raised by such men as Pym and Coke, but they were not finally settled in their time. The Petition of Right embodied the principle that in such matters Parliament was supreme, the Royal prerogative must not over-ride the powers entrusted to Parliament by the voice of the nation. This was all very well, but Stuart subtilty and intrigue managed to keep up the absolutism of the Monarch in some form, and, on many occasions, to thwart the will of the Commons. It is strange that this state of things was borne with until the end of the Stuart dynasty. A kind of halo seemed to surround that ill-starred house; more than once do we find popular feeling breaking out in its favour, and, in utter forgetfulness of old wrongs, displaying its willingness to allow it to overbear the counsels of the wise. Loyalty is an admirable virtue, but it appeared somewhat ridiculous in the obsequiousness with which it bent to James the Second, and the blind confidence it so long reposed in him. " The gentlemen`of England trusted King James," said William of Orange, " who was an enemy of their religion and their laws, and they will not trust me, by whom their religion and laws have been preserved." This was painfully true; but then William was not a Stuart, and it may have been due to this circumstance that the principle for which the Puritan party had fought so persistently, in the reign of Charles the First, was firmly established in William's reign and remains the law of England to this day. Sunderland, a man of conspicuous ability but doubtful character, succeeded in establishing the rule that all money Bills are under the control of the Commons, and that the Cabinet be chosen from the party that has the largest following in the House, and must be immediately responsible to the House.   No change of a more democratic character than this has ever been made in our constitution, or a change more significant of the growing spirit of liberty.   When Parliament assumed control of the purse, the Executive and the Army, the cause of the people was won.   But the wisdom of the English is not seen more in what it abolished, than in what it retained.   If it withdrew arbitrary power from the King, it did not touch the Crown itself ; except during the brief period of the Commonwealth and Protectorate, which in the long course of English history may properly be regarded as a parenthesis, however momentous its consequences, since it was quite off the lines of English tradition and law.   The

Second Chamber was also preserved. As a social and moral influence, as the fountain of honour, and the representative of the nation to foreign Powers in whose name the nation speaks, as the symbol of authority and unity the English Sovereign has never been more necessary to us than he is at present. In a different way the House of Lords is essential to our national well-being, safeguarding us against haste and incompleteness ; and, so far as a revising Chamber can, ensuring sobriety in our legislation. Nor is it now likely that any further great change will be made in our Constitution.

It would be well whenever and as often as we recall this period of our history, and the incidents which distinguished it, to associate with it the faithful and fearless men, who, at the risk of their lives and their liberties, inaugurated these beneficial changes and laid the foundations of the freedom we now enjoy.

To them fell the task of moulding the political thought of the nation, and they did it with such success that it is doubtful if any politician of modern times could bring himself to think in terms other than those shaped for him in that flowering time of liberty.

It may be alleged on the contrary that the facts do not all tally with these propositions. Was not the chief instrument in the Puritan revolt as great a despot in his way as any Tudor or Stuart ? Did not Oliver, in the interval of his rule, change the form of government at will, until he succeeded in making it in practice a one-man rule ; justifying his procedure in language scarcely distinguishable from that of Charles. This cannot be denied. It must also be granted that when a constitutional ruler opposes his counsellors and puts forward the apology that in going against the people's will he is seeking their good—which was in the main true of Cromwell, though not of Charles—it is impossible to give judgment in his favour. If, therefore, we were to take the Protector as the sole exponent of the politics of the Puritans, we should be forced to deny their right to be regarded as the originators of the freedom of Parliament. He found Parliament a thing to be endured, a cross to be borne, a hindrance to the realisation of his projects ; indeed, when we remember his naturally fiery temper, we may well marvel at the self-control which enabled him to keep its discordant elements so long together. But the best that can be said of him as the head of the State, in justification of his conduct, is that he was no Parliamentarian. He was deficient in the arts which go to make a successful political leader —suavity, patience, subtilty, dexterous handling of delicate questions and of men of perverse minds. As a matter of fact great military leadership and Parliamentary skill is so rare a combination we hardly dare look for it in any human being. Even our own great Duke, with all the prestige of Waterloo, as well as his own upright character, to commend him, cannot be regarded as a political success. The qualities which make for efficiency in the field are often those which bring disaster in the Senate. Cromwell was, in his day, the first military commander in Europe, but, in the Senate, we look to him in vain for those wiles and arts, with which Walpole and Pitt and Palmerston and Gladstone succeeded in leading men to see things as they saw them, and to commit themselves to courses which were often nothing more than hazardous adventures.

It is not then to Cromwell we turn when we think of political liberty. Pym, Hampden, Eliot, Coke, Milton, are the names which occur to our minds when we speak of " freedom broadening down from precedent to precedent." From their day to ours, the Commons has been slowly gaining in power, until it is now become absolute to the extent of causing some of its warmest friends to feel apprehensive of the future. The stream which began to flow when the Puritan leaders, with sincere expressions of loyalty to the throne, questioned the prerogatives claimed by James, has ever since kept on its course, with few interruptions, broadening and deepening as it flows, and the inevitable result has followed, which might have been foreseen : power which was once in the hands of a King is now transferred to the people, and Labour, commanding the largest following and a majority of votes, can do practically what it pleases. If the passion for righteousness which distinguished the nobler minds in the Puritan party in the seventeenth century dwells in the Labour party of the twentieth century, and its leaders are determined to profit by the mistakes of the men of the Commonwealth, the country need have no fear of its new masters. They may sometimes act rashly, but they will act justly, and England will be safer, happier, wealthier

E

in their hands than in the hands of an irresponsible Stuart. Our fear is that the growth of religious thought has not kept pace with the growth of political thought in the country; that the modern Puritan preachers, who are definitely in the line of succession of such men as Baxter among the Free Churches, and Usher in the English Church, have, to some extent, failed to keep the flame of Evangelical piety burning on the altar of the nation's heart.

This fear may be groundless; of one thing we may be well assured, and that is that the Rationalism to which Morley, with insufficient reason, attributes so much of our liberty, has no great hold on the labour element. Here and there you may find a Tom Paine, but you will far more often find a local preacher or Methodist prayer leader, an influence redolent of Oliver's camps, where the voice of prayer was rarely silent. Such men are the salt of the Labour party, which in no short time will be ruling the country; and if they are a majority in their party, and their influence paramount, all is right with England. They will see to it that justice is done to their own class, they will enlighten the ignorant and restrain the selfish elements in it, both of which are dangerously strong; and when they have learnt the position of that quiet middle class, the gentle poor, which at present has neither voice nor representation, and of whose existence they are hardly aware, there can be little doubt that their wrongs stand a better chance of being redressed at the hands of Labour than ever they have stood hitherto. This forecast rests, of course, upon the assumption and the hope that the Puritan spirit, which has never been quenched in the pious English working classes, since Bunyan wrote and Baxter preached, is still strong enough to influence political thought.

To the student of politics the experiment of another Puritan Parliament, for it will amount to that, must prove of absorbing interest. It will have no King, of the Stuart stamp, to thwart it, no Cromwell to hustle it ; possibly a House of Lords, with so little patrician and so much parvenu blood in it, may not be as sympathetic as the old nobility might have proved. It will start on its course with everything changed except its own undying spirit of righteousness—supposing it to be all that is here assumed—the spirit that lived in the great soul of Oliver, and which would have been manifested in every act of his political career, had not a cruel fate thrust the harder course upon him—the spirit of the Old Testament—from whose deep wells the Independents drank so freely—which commands us " to do justly and to love mercy and to walk humbly with God."

It is very unlikely that the originators of the opposition to the King foresaw to what lengths their action would lead the nation, but, if they took account of it, they must have realised that it could not stop with the claims made in the Petition of Right, important though these were. They must have known that they would have successors in the House who would continue and enlarge upon the policy begun by them.

> " Our echoes roll from soul to soul
> And go for ever and for ever."

What we have to concern ourselves with, however, is that a movement begun some three hundred years ago, by a small body of determined men, having taken its natural course, results in our day in placing unlimited powers upon the shoulders of the people. The nation definitely repudiates the dictum that " Those who think must govern those who toil," unless, indeed, we have come to the conclusion that the miner and the railway porter think as soundly and judge as justly as the best of men ; which of course may prove to be true. Meanwhile we must wait for the proof, and the experiment necessary for its production may occasion some pain and loss. Should the experiment succeed, we shall think of Pym and 1640, and bless his memory. Should it fail—well the country must see that it does not fail ; for in truth we have nothing to follow. We have tried every form of representation, and this is the last.

CHAPTER VII

EXPANSION OF ENGLAND UNDER PURITAN RULE

If Cromwell was not a successful Parliamentary hand, he was great, nevertheless, in statesmanship. England had fallen low as a European power under James and Charles; it made a noteworthy recovery under Cromwell. The Stuarts loved themselves; Oliver, like Elizabeth, loved England. It is only fair that all his policy, domestic and foreign, should be judged from this view-point. Whatever faults may be charged to him, let this stand to his credit, that as a great-hearted Englishman he sought England's good, temporal and spiritual. He followed and even improved upon Elizabeth's design of making the country a great maritime power. Ships of war and ships of commerce came in quick succession from every yard and graving-dock around the coast; Penn and Venables gave us Jamaica, the gem of the West Indies; Drake and Hawkins did not inspire more respect for the English flag than Cromwell's seamen won for it. In every Council Chamber of Europe it was felt advisable to court the goodwill of England; since it was recognised that the invincible Ironsides and the saucy sea-dogs could turn the scales in a trial of strength between any two powers. Mazarin and

Louis XIV. opened negotiations with Oliver, and found his great brain and his stout British heart quite a match for their crafty diplomacy ; though a day came when " the clever little Jack-anapes " at Versailles, whose conceit equalled his ambition, expressed deep regret that he had ever held intercourse with the regicide ; yet all the time his shrewdness must have taught him that while Oliver's star was in the ascendant, it was England's *siècle d'or*, not France's.

The one drawback to Cromwell's expansiveness was lack of money. You cannot make omelets without breaking eggs, and great operations, such as he engaged in, could not be carried out with an empty exchequer, and, Parliament being practically in abeyance, there was no way of re-plenishing it. The state of finance on the death of the Protector has often been made the grounds of a heavy indictment against his whole policy ; but this is manifestly unfair, for if Cromwell's enterprises had peace for their ultimate object, and commercial prosperity as the result of peace, then the attainment of such result was well worth the cost. If the fruit did not ripen in his day, and could not ripen in the deplorable days of the two last Stuarts, it has ripened since. Cromwell laboured and we have entered into his labour.

The purpose of the foregoing observations is to endeavour to establish the fact that Cromwell had a lofty conception of the position of England as not only a European but a world power ; that he aimed at making his country not only Godly but great, holding with unshaken conviction that its greatness could not stand apart from Godliness. He felt that this aim could not be attained unless we were strong on land and sea, and he set himself to revive the policy of Elizabeth by making England Mistress of the Seas ; a policy that has been followed up by great English statesmen ever since, and will possibly never be departed from, for it has entered deeply into the thought of the whole nation.

In domestic affairs, not less than foreign, Cromwell showed his greatness, though all must admit the accuracy of Clarendon's statement that " his greatness at home was but a shadow of the glory he had abroad." If Blake swept the seas and wrenched the trident from the Dutch, establishing England in a position it has never finally lost, as the first sea-power in the world ; " if France, Spain, Portugal, Pope and Princes of Italy, bowed to the summons of Oliver,"[1] we must not allow these triumphs of arms and diplomacy to overshadow the Protector's successes in consolidating the empire at home and making it something much more than an United Kingdom in name. What he might have thought of certain sentimental proposals for separate Parliaments and Executives within that kingdom, supposing it possible that they could have been mooted in his time, we cannot say ; but we may with certainty assert that to any proposal which might even seem to menace Protestantism, which to his judgment was the *raison d'etre* of English

---

[1] Harrison's " Cromwell," p. 209.

Christianity, he would not have given place; no, not for an hour.

The contrast between his age and ours is striking. Had we been amongst those who heard his first rugged speech in Parliament we might well have asked, " Lord, what shall this man do ? " All the outstanding features which marked that age have changed or disappeared. Feudalism is buried; the Divine right of Kings is gone; the theory no Bishop, no Church, dissolves in the dry light of history and under the test of experience; Parliament is free, the will of the people supreme; and England stands forth as the greatest military and naval kingdom in the world, great in commerce, great in art and literature, greatest of all as an advocate of righteousness and a friend of the oppressed and the weak. It would be absurd to attribute all this to Oliver, and those who stood nearest to him, but it was all in his heart; and as he and the wiser and more reasonable men, in that strangely mixed party we call Puritan, thought in their day, so England thinks to-day.

Expansion, therefore, is not to be measured by what is acquired outside a kingdom's natural boundaries; expansion may and should proceed at home, and upon this the mind of the Protector was set far more than upon territorial aggrandisement. His practical mind saw that for the promotion of home expansion, the first thing to be aimed at was peace and order; these attained, the rest was sure to follow. Many of Oliver's friendly critics have compared him to a parish

constable armed with a truncheon, putting down
disorder and setting every one in his proper place ;
a description which fits him very well. The constable's hand was by no means light, but it made
a way for trade, commerce, justice, learning and
internal rest. " Property, wealth, harmony were
restored to the nation." Peace, retrenchment
and reform are the well-worn election cries of the
political party of modern times, which has most
in common with the religious ideas of the Puritans,
and, whether borrowed from Oliver or not, they
certainly represent most truly his social aims, and
afford another of the many proofs we possess
that Puritan ideals, far from perishing with the
Commonwealth, have found a permanent home
in the country. Apart from the quarrels and
unrest in Parliament the land enjoyed great peace,
and gradually recovered that confidence which
is the mainspring of trade prosperity. In a
very short time, we are told, the old spirit of
personal loyalty to a Sovereign was replaced by
the new spirit of duty to the State. Can we doubt
that this was occasioned by the knowledge men
gathered of the high character of the State's
rulers ? " For the first and only time in modern
Europe," writes a recent biographer, " morality
and religion became the sole qualification insisted on by the Court. In the whole history of
modern Europe, Oliver is the one ruler into whose
presence no vicious man could come, whose service no vicious man might enter."[1] Such praise
as this had never been given to an English crowned

---

[1] Harrison's " Cromwell," p. 208.

head. In the Protector's case it was richly deserved, for it was nothing but the naked truth. This, let it be borne in mind, is a description of a Court of the middle of the seventeenth century; but how modern it appears, and how close is its resemblance to a Court that would commend itself to what we are accustomed to speak of as " the Nonconformist conscience ? " It is all very well to scoff at the Nonconformist conscience, which at times, no doubt, can be as overbearing and unpractical as the Roundhead preacher, but, given its due, it has stood on many occasions on the side of righteousness when that side was far from popular. It denounced slavery and helped to bring about its downfall, it advocated abstinence from alcohol, and the prohibition of the trade amongst the native races of Africa and the East, and its restriction at home; it hated the opium traffic with a perfect hatred; it favoured a system of national education, a restful Sabbath, a contented working class, comfortably housed and reasonably remunerated for its toil; it has ever been the friend of peace and the opponent of unjust wars. Well; the Nonconformist conscience is a Puritan legacy, the tradition has come down unbroken through quite ten generations of Christian Englishmen, and on the whole has been of great benefit to the country. Occasionally the conscience has been drugged through a prejudiced alliance with a political party in the State, a subtle self-deception leading it to a persuasion that a course is right because it wishes to believe it right. But that it can recover and prove itself worthy of its honourable origin has been demonstrated in our recent troubles, when the whole of Nonconformist England—we may overlook the conscientious objector—stood a solid phalanx on the side of King and Parliament, and gave of its best on the fields of France and Flanders in the cause of liberty and justice. If, then, we recognise that, with some reservations, "the despised thing" has been good, that it has done much to sweeten the social atmosphere and to set men's minds on righteousness, it would be ungrateful on our part to forget the rock from which Nonconformity was hewn, or, if we will, the channel through which it has flowed down to us.

Granting that we are indebted in large measure to the Commonwealth and its great head, for such benefits as are here indicated, abiding reforms and great ethical principles which coloured thought and influenced conduct for many years, we may well pause for a moment to give a glance at the difficulties under which Cromwell held his ground and propagated his principles. It is well known that Charles had offered a reward for anyone who would assassinate him. Though such a proposal may shock us, it need not cause wonder; but that men of his own party should be conspirators, with his and their enemies, in plots to take away his life is painful to contemplate. Anabaptists and Fifth Monarchy men were as full of hatred of Oliver as Charles himself, perhaps even more full, for Charles though he would gladly see his rival put out of the way was anything but a

good hater. Nor was this all. Probably the
greatest Puritan of his time, or of any time, was
Richard Baxter, yet so attached was Baxter to
the ancient constitution of England and so greatly
did he abhor the execution of the King, he found
language hardly adequate to express his indig-
nation at "the regicide and the usurper." He
meditated the detachment of his own regiment,
of which he was chaplain, from the cause, and,
should fortune favour his scheme, all the generals
of the army from their leader. The device of
course failed, but Baxter did not fail even then to
raise his voice publicly against what he described
as "the treason, rebellion, perfidiousness and
hypocrisy" of Cromwell.

There is much truth in the saying that "the
man under the lamp gets the least light." Baxter
was too near the Protector to form an impartial
judgment, and with all his excellences he had a
stubborn will and strong prejudices, prejudices
which did not incline him favourably towards
his patron; he must also have been well aware
that Cromwell gave him anything but a cordial
welcome amongst his troops. We get perhaps a
more judicial estimate from Sir James Stephen,
whose knowledge of both men, gathered from
many different quarters, was quite exceptional,
and who sums up Cromwell's character in the
pregnant sentences "there were many worse
men, and few greater."

Much more might be written on this point,
but enough has been said to illustrate Cromwell's difficult position, and the risks he ran in

freeing his own age from its many troubles, and enriching the ages which came after him, by pointing out the path of freedom and laying the foundation of domestic peace and trade prosperity.

CHAPTER VIII

THE INFLUENCE OF PURITAN HOME LIFE

ATTENTION has already been directed to the
effects of character on national politics, and since
character is and must be a home growth, like
plants raised from seeds in shelter before planting
out, it is necessary to glance at the domestic and
social life of the Puritan, before we can understand
the extraordinary power of the movement in the
nation and in the churches.

It must be granted that on the religious side
there was an awful severity, not only in regard to
what was deemed soundness of doctrine but in
the administration of discipline, a severity which
was enforced with even greater rigour by the
settlers in New England than by the Sectaries in
the Mother Country, though the extreme Independent left little to complain of on that score in
either place. Hawthorne's "Scarlet Letter" is
no overdrawn picture of the terrible consequences
attached to a lapse from virtue on the part of
a Church member. The Church pitiless, the
sinner hopeless, bearing the brand of shame
until death gave the grand release, present to
us a picture in violent and heartless contrast to
the mercy and tenderness of Him who said to one,
charged with a like transgression, "neither do I

condemn thee; go, and sin no more." Yet when
our thoughts revert to the English Court, and the
state of morals amongst the Cavaliers of the
seventeenth century, the question is forced on us
"Is there not a cause?" Milton closes his
Comus with the noble words, "Love virtue, she
alone is free." And, as evidence of the lasting
impression Puritan views on this subject have
made on the inhabitants of both countries, it is a
fact, patent to all who take the pains to inquire
into it, that sexual immorality, especially con-
jugal infidelity, is a vice as rare as it is revolting
in devout Puritan families of our time. No other
vice leaves behind it such a train of sadness and
shame. It is, of course, a delicate question of
casuistry whether or not this view be sound; or,
putting it in another way, whether there is not a
danger that, in laying exceptional emphasis on
one commandment of the immortal decalogue, we
may weaken the solemn force of the remainder.
A fitting answer to such questionings is, perhaps,
furnished by the prevalence of divorce in America,
and the clamour for more of it in England; for
although the people who take advantage of
divorce law, are as far removed from "the Godly"
of the twentieth century, as Buckingham and
Rochester were from Baxter and George Fox, yet
the preservation of a sound moral opinion, in
however small a circle, must exercise a wholesome
and restraining influence on the public mind
generally.

America is prolific in the production of strange
adjectives, and, just at present, one of the most

familiar to our ears is the word " dry." That so
many of the States are advocating, and even
accepting, the condition of " dryness," that is the
total prohibition of the sale of alcohol within their
borders, may strike a Hedonist as an amusing
absurdity, yet it is a most remarkable proof of
the persistence of Puritan principles. It is a well-
known fact, related in Traill's " Social England "
and Gardiner's " History of the Commonwealth,"
that, even under the Stuart dynasty, Puritan
influence was so strong, in some English counties,
almost all the ale-houses were shut up by order
of the magistrates ; and, under the Commonwealth,
brewers, some of them men of high character and
enjoying much popularity, could not gain a seat on
the magistrates' bench, or be appointed mayor of
a borough. Here, then, we have one of those
singular illustrations of the mingling of politics
and religion, which was so marked a feature of
the Puritan movement, and which has never
altered with the lapse of time, except, indeed, to
become more prominent. In the particular instance just referred to, the English Puritan has
made many futile attempts to follow his American
brother. So long as he was willing to confine
himself to moral suasion, he won not only respect,
but a remarkable amount of success ; but his hope
of making England " dry " seems as remote as
ever it has been ; nor can we feel assured that the
policy, in the United States, will ultimately fare
any better than those earlier attempts of the
English Puritans to enforce their ideals of morals
and manners and religious observances upon this

country by legislative action. But that the policy is popular with a large section of the American public and is, for the moment at least, strenuously pressed forward by able and intelligent advocates, is interesting as showing that the Puritan spirit is still a force to be reckoned with, and capable of making a deep impression on the thought of the Republic.

Thrift was another virtue seriously cultivated in Puritan families. Many a home was a miniature factory in which yarn was spun and durable material woven, chiefly by the pious Flemings who fled the sword of Alva, was worked up into wearing apparel, of a highly attractive appearance, though always adapted to the modest demeanour of the Puritan housewife or maiden. Cookery, and a knowledge of medicinal plants, such as camomile, dandelion and hoarhound ; brewing elder wine ; skill in the dressing of wounds and poulticing, were the common possession of every well-trained Puritan woman, a possession which proved of inestimable value during the Civil War, when it was turned to good account—one faithful daughter dressing the wounds of over three score Cromwellian soldiers in a day, and, in the midst of it, receiving the intelligence that her faithless lover had given his heart to another woman, and taken her to wife, which caused, we are told, but a very brief interruption to her work of mercy. " Since he hath made himself unworthy of my love, he is unworthy my anger or concern," was her philosophic reflection. She soon found a better mate. The men of the party were equally noted

F

for their industry, and not infrequently for their parsimony. The opinion has been put forward, and with much justification, that the great prosperity of England, as a trading and commercial nation, must be attributed to the ingrained habits of industry and thrift of the inhabitants of our British homes in those years of Puritan ascendency.

How grave a responsibility must therefore rest on the men who, by a lavish expenditure of public money, help to destroy those estimable habits, and to undermine the spirit of self-reliance, and even of self-respect, which Puritanism inculcated and fostered to the utmost limit of its power.

Before passing from the subject of thrift, it is necessary to allude to a group of institutions, the strongest and in some respects the most beneficial to the working classes in our country, the Friendly Societies. Some seven of these occupy positions of great importance; one of them, The Manchester Unity of Oddfellows, possessing a capital of over eighteen millions, the accumulated savings of our English working people; others, such as the Foresters and the Rechabites, holding strong financial positions, while several smaller organisations are thoroughly solvent and confer many benefits on their members. The Insurance Act, which is not yet ten years old, has done much to weaken the position of these societies, and, what is a much more serious matter, tends to undermine the strong, self-reliant spirit of the working classes, which up to the passing of that Act had the full management of their contributions in their own hands. A Government audit, and even a

Government subsidy, might have been welcomed, leaving the management, as it had been, wholly in the hands of the members. Unfortunately our politicians were not content to stop there, but must set up a vast system of organisation, outside the societies, at enormous expense to the nation, and to the great injury of that independence and personal initiative which had hitherto been the pride and glory of the British workman. The subject is introduced here, however, not for the purpose of criticising the Government, whose good intention we need not doubt, but in order to direct attention to the fact that these Friendly Societies are the direct result of the habits of thrift inherited from our Puritan ancestors ; that they have been founded and worked by the Puritans of modern England—the sturdy, Godly, sober working men, for the most part radicals in politics and dissenters in religion ; and that the members of the National Church, who share their fortunes in these organisations, and have joined them in large numbers, share also their religious opinions, just as Puritan Churchmen of the Stuart period had much in common with the views of men like Baxter. Indirectly the influence of the Friendly Societies on religion, politics and social order has been very great.

The strength of character, of which the habits of those people was the result, must be sought for in the piety of the home. Never, since the Christian faith first found its way to England, has home piety flourished so greatly amongst us as in the palmy days of Puritanism. In the absence or the illness of the "good man," the British matron was found as ready an expounder of the Word as her lord. Bunyan tells of the pious and devout expositions of a group of Godly women which reduced him to silence and a deep humility, so far did their spiritual experiences and inward light surpass his poor attainments. The morning and evening religious exercises were long, the Old Testament Scriptures were in high favour, the wars of Joshua being relieved by comforting lections from " the sweet Psalmist of Israel " ; metrical psalms, without instrumental accompaniment, were sung and prayers of inordinate length offered. Yet, dull and wearisome as all this sounds to us, comfort and edification were thereby supplied to the spirits of the worshippers in those homes, and that type of character created which, by and bye, was to make the army of the New Model, the pride of Oliver's heart and the dread of his enemies. On Sundays no Puritan absented himself from the meeting-house, where often the sermon lasted for two hours, and the preacher exerted himself to such purpose he must sometimes change his shirt after his discourse. Indeed, one divine is said to have been so affected by his own sermons that he wept profusely, and on one occasion as many as six napkins had been known to be hardly sufficient to dry his tears, whereat the congregation was greatly moved.

Criticise those times as we may, they produced a race of men renowned for Godliness, honesty, sobriety and valour ; and women of such piety, chastity, modesty and homeliness as England had never previously known, and it is doubtful if England will ever look upon their like again.

Did ever Christian woman excel Margaret Charlton, that lady of gentle birth, "rich in gifts of nature and of fortune," who became the young wife of the middle-aged Baxter, to whom she owed her soul? When the prelates, of whom Coleridge wrote, "God forbid I should seek to justify them as Christians," had had their way with Baxter, and he is cast out of the Church, and cast into prison, her gentle ministrations, soothing, cheering, comforting him, sharing his lot, made his prison cell a home of light and peace. And if few Puritan women equalled her, many resembled her, for with justice Gardiner dwells on "the mingled strength and sweetness in the character of the womanhood of England, nurtured in the great Protestant tradition." [1]

But had those worthies no amusements, no human pastimes to break the monotony of a life such as we are describing, and to answer to their lighter moods? This question will receive a fuller answer in another chapter; here let it suffice to say that of literature, such as might find a welcome in the homes of the industrial classes and stricter Sectaries, there was practically none. Bunyan's works, which would have entertained as well as improved the sober-minded, were a later product; and the novel had not yet come to birth, nor, if born, could it hope for a cordial reception. Tracts by Baxter, Buchanan and Milton, and sermons by leading Puritan divines, were

---

[1] "History of England," VII., p. 340.

available ; sacred verse by George Herbert, Quarles, or later by Henry Vaughan, were all of this age, as well as the incomparable lighter poetry of Robert Herrick ; but it is doubtful how much, if any, of those, with the exception of the strictly Puritan productions, found their way into the hands of those serious-minded folk. The Bible, sacred songs and psalms, and the harpsichord, imported from the famous Ruckers of Antwerp, were deemed almost sufficient, even in many a wealthy Puritan home, to meet the æsthetic and literary tastes of the young. But the needle and the distaff were seldom idle ; spinning yarn, working samplers, stitching household garments, brewing and baking, cultivating herbs and flowers, and keeping the home sweet and spotlessly clean, left little time for the pursuit of vanities. Yet while the log blazed on the open hearth and the rushlight threw a gentle glow over the scene, many a soft glance passed between some " Mistress Marjorie " and her young lover, and often another yarn was spun, to the buzz of her spinning wheel, than that which seemed to engage her whole attention, as her neatly-shaped foot kept time to the movement and her deft hand arranged the passage of the threads. On the whole neither youth nor maiden, of that interesting period, stand in need of posthumous sympathy. They had their ways of enjoying life, simpler than ours, but not on that account less real and satisfactory.

Times have changed since those days, but hearts are still the same, and the men and women whose manner of life we are considering have transmitted to us thoughts and principles which, though now expressed in language and habit different from theirs, will live while England lives.

In considering our indebtedness to the Puritans, it should never be forgotten by those who value English home life that they gave it to us. " Home, as we conceive it now," writes J. R. Green, " was the creation of the Puritan." If Puritanism occasioned the " loss of the passion, the caprice; the subtle and tender play of feeling, the breadth of sympathy, the quick pulse of delight " of the Elizabethan age, " on the other hand life gained in moral grandeur, in a sense of the dignity of manhood, in orderliness and equitable force. The larger geniality of the age that had passed away was replaced by an intense tenderness within the narrower circle of the home." Gravity and seriousness reigned there, softened and warmed by family love, until the home of the honest, upright Englishman has become the sweetest and purest thing on earth :

> " A quiet centre in a troubled world,
> A haven where the rough winds whistle never,
> And the still sails are in the sunbeams furled."

CHAPTER IX

WHILE it is undeniable that religion influences politics, it is equally true that it is itself much influenced by art. The England which confronted the opening of the twentieth century was an England mainly created by Puritan influences, but those influences had broadened, and attained a completeness lacking in the days of the Commonwealth. The tolerant spirit inherited from the Protector and the Army, which embraced all forms of faith except Prelacy and Popery, had in the meantime enlarged its scope to such an extent that Prelatists and Romanists and Free Churchmen were to be found everywhere acting together for the common good of the nation, and, with the exception of the Romanist, frequently worshipping together. There can be little doubt that the growth of this better feeling had been largely aided, indirectly and perhaps unconsciously, by what may be described as the re-birth in the country of the artistic temperament, and the thirst for good literature amongst the sober-minded in all classes of society. To these two influences, art and literature, acting together as a great healing and moderating force, rather than to Lord Morley's idea of the growing spirit of Rationalism,

we owe it that the Puritanism of the seventeenth
century, which was marked with an asperity and
a sternness, which was of the age rather than of
the movement, has shaded off into a Puritanism of
culture and reasonableness that has blessed and
still blesses the nation by furnishing it "with
sweeter manners, purer laws." The Puritan of to-
day, in all essentials, stands where his ancestors
stood. It is true that, unlike them, he is rarely
Calvinistic in doctrine, but a free Parliament, a
free people, a constitutional King, are, in politics,
the very breath of his nostrils, be he Whig or Tory ;
while the divine right of Kings is for him a dead
question ; and the maxim " no Bishop, no Church,"
no longer troubles his dreams, whether he belong
to an Episcopal community or not. Like the
great Tudor divines of Edward VI.'s time, he
sees no harm in a moderate Episcopacy ; but just
because he is conscious of life in himself and life
in his Church, when it has no Bishop, he refuses
to identify life with external organisation of any
sort.

It may with confidence be said that these are
the views held to-day, by a majority of the English
people so overwhelming that those of a contrary
mind are not to be accounted of. The Oxford
movement, begun some eighty years ago, though
it gave us the poetry and piety of Keble, the
learning of Pusey, and many lives of exceptional
beauty and holiness, utterly failed in its scarcely
veiled attempt to overthrow Puritanism and may
now be regarded, outside the ranks of the Clergy
and the Convocations, as a spent force. Even

there its aspect has changed greatly from the
sobriety and orderliness of its founders. The
splendour and costliness of its ritual, deeply im-
pressive though it be to some minds, is to others
a sure sign of decaying strength ; for " religious
and moral ideas," writes Lecky, " resemble the
sun, whose last rays possessing little heat spend
themselves in creating beauty."

Secularism is the most dangerous enemy Puritanism has had to meet, for secularism makes war on
the Bible and the Sabbath, the two buttresses of
Puritanism ; on the Bible more largely by neglect
of it than by ridicule or criticism ; on the Sabbath
by ministering to the love of pleasure.

Mr. Gladstone spoke truly when he said that
the English character owed almost everything to
the English Sunday and the English Bible ; and
we know that he himself honoured and made full
use of both. So strict was he in his observance
of public worship—" a twicer," he called himself—
and so devout a student of the Scriptures, that
not inaptly may he be described as a high-Church
Puritan. The lovers and friends of a Puritan
England, who would preserve their good inheritance for the nation, should wisely devote themselves to the encouraging of a more joyous use
of the Book and of the Day. " Were I cast on a
desert island," said an old soldier, " where I could
find means of subsistence, with a Bible, Shakespeare
and the Pilgrim's Progress, as my companions,
I doubt if I could ever have a dull hour." As
regards Sunday, the surest way to win it back as
a day of rest and worship, which is the Puritan

ideal, is to clothe it with such festival brightness
as will make it the happiest day in the week ; and
it may surprise some who have formed their opinions
of a Puritan Sabbath from the action of rigid
Presbyterian Magistrates and Ana-Baptists of the
Commonwealth period, that Lucy Hutchinson,
and Cromwell himself, took this more wholesome
view of the day of rest, and would have it observed
not as a day of gloom, but hail it in Herbert's
words :

> " Oh, day most calm, most bright,
> The week were dark but for thy light."

In some respects the Free Church Puritan has
left Oliver's path ; for Charles, who used the
Church as the instrument of his own despotism,
was not a more thorough-going Erastian than
Oliver, who upheld the opinion that "the care
of religion was the duty of the State." He also
laboured unweariedly to create an united kingdom.
"It was his armed right hand," says Morley,
"that crushed the absolutist pretensions alike of
crown and mitre, and then forced the three kingdoms into the mould of a single state." In both
these matters many are inclined to believe that
Cromwell's judgment was sounder than that of
modern Radical Puritanism. A Church co-extensive with the State, with the State as equal
partner, is sure to be more tolerant, and to that
extent more Christian, than a Church autonomous
and sectarian ; and the solid unity of the British
Isles, with one Parliament and one Executive,
seems to be a safer method of rule, and more
conducive to prosperity and national security,

than any alternative that has so far been proposed.
Pitt's methods of consolidation may have been as
open to criticism as Cromwell's, but in neither
case has the result been a failure. With such
readjustments of thought and practice as are here
mentioned, Puritanism remains faithful to its
first faith. But it will be said by some objector,
if later Puritanism has yielded to the influences
of art and literature, how can it possibly claim
affinity with the Puritanism which banned Marlowe,
Ben Jonson, Shakespeare and even Herrick;
denounced Masques and Plays, broke down the
exquisitely carved images, and dashed to pieces
the stained glass figures in our Churches? If
Digby called Wentworth "the grand apostate of
the Commonwealth," what shall we call the men
who would build to-day what their fathers destroyed?

The best hound may miss its quarry should it
start on and follow a wrong scent, and nothing
is easier than to delude a whole nation of readers,
if the first writer in the field raises a false issue
or distorts facts under his hand or only states the
half of them. On the other hand, it is a great
art, in studying a movement, to discriminate
between what is permanent and what is transitory
in it.

Puritanism, as we have seen, is " a word of many
shades." The Baptists and the Fifth Monarchy
men were ruthless iconoclasts. Smashing windows
and images and burning books of " carnal lore,"
" the spawn of hell," was light work to men who
thought they would render God service by staining

their hands with the blood of no less a person
than the Protector himself. There were others of
a milder cast who in their zeal for purity disliked
the emblems of "popery and prelacy" to such
an extent that they resolved to have them down.
In their honest minds there was a burning hatred
of falsehood of any kind. "They would have no
lies in the Churches," says Froude, "either in the
pulpits or in the windows." And truly many of
the so-called saints had small title to saintliness,
and many of the real saints could have borne no
possible resemblance to the figures which represented them. St. John, for instance, a Galilean
fisherman, would have been more truly presented
to the worshipping public in sea-boots and a rough
jersey, and a face tanned by sea and sun than as
an effeminate creature with a soft girlish face and,
a white, flowing garment.[1] The sons of Zebedee
did not go afloat in such ridiculous habiliments.
And so our Puritan made up his mind that if the
"Son of Thunder" had not justice done to him,
far better his image should perish; and in this
he was more honest than the artist, though, it
must be confessed, in a matter of so small importance zeal over-reached itself.

But there was a very large and powerful body

---

[1] To my readers and to the Editor of *Punch* I owe an
apology for yielding to the temptation to insert the following
lines :—

" I don't know who Saint Mawes was, but he surely can't
    have been
A stiff old stone gazebo on a carved cathedral screen ;
Or a holy-looking customer, rigged out in blue and red,
In a sunset-coloured window, with a soup-plate round his
    head."

in the Puritan party, strong in their attachment to the principles of religious and political liberty, who never shared the views or approved the rough deeds of the extremists. The men and women composing this body were the salt of Puritanism and represented its best and most permanent elements. It is a vulgar error to describe the movement in terms only suitable to the least attractive characters in it, but it is an error which unfortunately has long held the field and is become the common possession of the greater part of Europe. " Such false logic did the children of darkness use to argue with against the hated children of light, whom they branded besides as illiterate, morose, melancholy, discontented, crazed, sort of men, not fit for human conversation; as such they made them not only the sport of the pulpit, which was become but a more solemn sort of stage, but every stage, and every table, and every puppet-show, belched forth profane scoffs upon them, the drunkards made them their songs, and all fiddlers and mimics learned to abuse them, as finding it the most gainful way of fooling."[1]

Here we have from the pen of a sane contemporary, a Puritan of Puritans, the case stated from the other side. It was a clever device on the part of enemies, whose aim was to discredit and cast reproach on the whole movement, to pick out its unlovely features and its repulsive characters, and present them in exaggerated form as properly descriptive of the whole. The device has succeeded only too well, and colours the

---

[1] Memoirs of Colonel Hutchinson.

thought of the nation to this day. The true facts wear a very different appearance. What sort of man was Cromwell, for example, in his home ? We know the pious atmosphere of that house, the high standard of moral conduct, the stainless honour, the just rule, the prayerful solicitude of the mother for her great son. But the son was no sour-faced ascetic. Like Bunyan he had his moods of deepest melancholy. They were fashionable, and they were transient. He loved a good horse ; and few squires in Hunting-donshire were better judges of one ; he rode to hounds, he hawked, he delighted in good music, and cheerful company. At Whitehall his hos-pitality was princely ; and if a long grace preceded and a psalm followed the meal, all the more honour to the man for bearing as " godly a car-riage " in the seats of the mighty as he bore on his homely farm. Baxter describes him as " of a sanguine complexion, naturally of such a vivacity, hilarity, and alacrity as another man hath when he hath drunken a cup too much."

On the other hand it must not be forgotten that most of the great houses of the Country party, later known as the Whigs, if not definitely attached to the Puritans, sympathised with them ; to some extent politically, more largely religiously.[1]

---

[1] At the beginning of the reign of Elizabeth's successor, the bulk of the country gentlemen, the bulk of the wealthy traders had become Puritans. In the first Parliament of James the House of Commons refused, for the first time, to transact business on a Sunday. His second Parliament chose to receive the Communion at St. Margaret's Church instead of Westminster Abbey, " for fear of copes and wafer-cakes."— Green's " History of the English People," vol. VII.

It would be absurd to think of those " broad-shouldered, genial Englishmen," and their high born dames, frowning on the simple enjoyments of their tenants and retainers, or themselves declining the pleasures of the chase and the table and the common pastimes of country life.

Lucy Hutchinson came of a good English stock. Her father, Sir Allen Apsley, was Lieutenant of the Tower, and all her early associations were Puritan. " By the time I was four years old," she writes, " I could read English perfectly, and having a great memory I was carried to hear sermons, and while I was very young could remember and repeat them exactly." She also read Latin in which she excelled her brothers. So far well ; but what will the man who believes that every Puritan condemned all the arts and graces as " works of the flesh and the devil " say to her next sentences ? " I had, at one time," she continues, " eight tutors in several qualities ; languages, music, dancing, writing and needle-work." To writing and needlework there will be no objection, but a Puritan maiden—who remembered and repeated sermons—with her lute and her harpsichord and her dancing master, must come as a very unwelcome piece of news to a mind made up to believe that sourness and Puritanism are convertible terms ; and all the more so when it is added that little Lucy was no exception, every Puritan child in a similar station in life had imposed upon her like pomps and vanities.

In Colonel Hutchinson we have the picture of a Puritan gentleman of great attractiveness, and we may conclude from it that there must have been many like him in those times. He played several instruments with skill, he dressed with taste, he sang, he fenced, he rode, he hawked, he directed the studies of his children, which included modern languages and the classics. He sought out London artists and encouraged them. Like Cromwell he acquired for the nation, some choice paintings and became a general patron of art. Pictures sold and given to their servants by the Stuarts were repurchased and preserved to the country. The passage in his memoirs under this head is so interesting some portions of it may here be transcribed for the reader's pleasure :—

" Paintings, sculptures, gravings, were considered by him, insomuch that he became a great virtuoso and patron of ingenuity. Being loth that the land should be disfurnished of all the rarities that were in it, whereof many were set for sale from the King's and diverse noblemen's collections, he laid out about two thousand pounds, in the choicest pieces of painting, most of which were bought out of the King's goods, which had been given to his servants to pay their wages. . . .

As he had a great delight, so he had a great judgment in music, and advanced his children's practice more than their tutors, he was also a great supervisor of their learning, and indeed was himself a tutor to them all. He spared not any cost for the education of both his sons and daughters in languages, sciences, music, dancing and all other qualities befitting their father's house."

If Colonel Hutchinson's had been the only Puritan home in England in which these accomplishments were cultivated, it might be said a single instance proves nothing. But even that we must not admit, for surely it proves that one can be a conscientious, devout Puritan, and yet a lover of all that is noble and beautiful in art,

G

mentally invigorating in literature, useful and interesting in science and philosophy. But we are safe in assuming that, in every county in England, Puritan homes existed enjoying, if not the same measure of culture, at least such a measure of it as corresponded to their abilities and lay within their reach. It is there we must look for the roots of the Puritanism that still flourishes in England, and maintains itself in unabated strength amongst Anglo-Saxon peoples, in kingdoms and dominions far over the seas.

There also do we find the explanation of the moderation which tempers our politics, and of that more reasonable spirit in religion which counts art as an handmaid, and not an enemy, of which the spirit of God is the inspirer, and is therefore to be rescued from degradation and consecrated to the highest service man can render.

" Craftsman's art and music's measure
For thy pleasure doth combine."

CHAPTER X

HOW PURITANISM AFFECTED POLITICS AND RELIGION IN SCOTLAND AND IRELAND

A GENERAL survey of Anglo-Saxon countries, in which we may include America, would present to us at the present hour a spectacle of many peoples amongst whom the Puritan political ideals had settled permanently and the religious ideals had weakened. But let it be observed that this weakening of the religious instinct is by no means confined to communities of the Puritan type. All over the world of Christendom, Catholic and Protestant communities alike, are, for the moment, losing ground ; and in the opinion of many wise observers, things will not mend until institutional Christianity, under every form, is remade from top to bottom. Apart from other considerations, and they are numerous, as to how this state of things has come about, account must be taken of the work of theological and historical experts ; work which has produced results which some of the experts little dreamed of. The critical study of the Bible and of early Church History has made a silent revolution in the minds of educated men, on such subjects as the meaning and limits of inspiration, and the organisation of the Christian Church. The matter would not be referred to here were the question not forced on us, how much or how little have Puritan influences had to do with this change, or have they any relation to it at all ? If we judged Puritanism, once and for all, by the rigorists of the seventeenth century or by the actions of the first New England Settlers, no place could be found for change, progress or variety of any description, but judged by the larger and more tolerant spirit of Milton, Hutchinson, Baxter and Cromwell himself, we arrive at the contrary view, that progress, change and adaptation were inevitable, and were really latent in the movement. Scotland affords a most striking illustration of this fact. Scotland, as we have already seen, at a very early stage of our internal troubles accepted the doctrinal position of Puritanism and, notwithstanding differences and misunderstandings with Oliver and his party, of a political character, differences so great as to lead to overtures to Charles on the part of Scotland, with the view of bringing him back, the people have remained steadfast to the Protestant faith. It is not necessary to travel over the familiar ground of Scottish history in this period. On the one hand, national feeling, always strong in Scotland, disposed the country favourably to the Stuarts ; on the other, Puritan principles and, we fear we must in justice add, bitter experience had begotten a feeling of the strongest antipathy to Prelacy.

Such facts are sufficient to explain a great many things in the history of that remarkable country, which are not very easily apprehended

by outsiders. Perhaps in no country in Europe
has religion played a more important part or
exercised so profound an influence on the course
of politics, finally resulting in leaving the land
Puritan in religion and predominantly Whiggish
in politics. At the same time Scotland has in
some respects changed more than any other
portion of the Empire. Presbyterianism in its
early days was an ecclesiastical despotism, yet it
took firm root amongst a people whose political
tendencies were essentially democratic. Its rapid
extension is to be accounted for by the
fact that, paradoxical as the statement may
seem, the despotism of the Church was itself
democratic, in the sense that it rested on the
goodwill of the people. To this circumstance
it was due that it found in the Scottish character,
which it strengthened and ennobled, a congenial
soil, and made a deep and abiding impression on
political thought. The independence of thought,
which was thus bred and fostered in political
circles, in process of time invaded the domain of
religion. The temper of mind which moved
Melville to call King James, " God's silly vassal,"
and to assure him that no earthly ruler could
claim authority over the conscience of a Christian
man, whose first allegiance must be ·to the
heavenly King, though in truth a political proposition of first importance, is just as truly a
religious proposition ; for we may assume that
the conscience which refused to be bound by a
King which men saw, would more readily refuse
perpetual submission to a tradition which they

had not seen. If the ministers of the National Church of Scotland, by which title of Church we understand the sum total of Scottish Presbyterians, are, as many believe, the ablest preachers and the most learned and liberal-minded divines in the kingdom; if Scotsmen are the most independent and clear-headed politicians we can boast of, all this may be put down to the circumstance of their carrying out, to a fuller extent than any others, the Puritan doctrine that politics are a chief interest of Christian men, that in fact religion and politics must not be separated in a Christian country, and secondly that the Christian conscience must be free, in other words the right of private judgment. It is true Covenants and Confessions seem to put a limit to such freedom, but they have not prevented the free expression of theological opinions, by men of sound learning and balanced judgment, which the first generation of Puritans would neither have understood nor tolerated. On the other hand so independent is the Scottish political mind, no wooer of the suffrages of a North British constituency can hope for election unless he is, or can persuade the electors that he is, a perfect reflection of their opinions and aspirations. The most eloquent and popular politician the House of Commons has known for three generations, was obliged to alter his address to a body of Scottish electors, at the instance of his own Committee, because of the unpopularity of a proposal which he had inserted in it, actually with the view of winning larger support. He was assured that his eloquence, his prestige, his great name, would count for nothing if that proposal stood.

Since Puritanism has held the field in Scotland, for more than three hundred years, we must place to its credit not only the conversion of the Highland clans, from a wild and ignorant rabble, into a highly intelligent and thoughtful population, but also the admirable spirit of independence in politics and the progressive thought in religion which are the most characteristic features of the Scotland of our day. Scotland in John Knox's day was backward and poverty stricken. That great man, more than any other, awakened the soul of the nation ; and the doctrines which he preached, with a tongue of fire, and with gestures so violent it seemed as if he must " dab the pulpit into blads " made the humblest shepherd or fisherman feel himself a man. We need not wonder then that Puritan principles, both religious and political, soon flooded the northern kingdom ; and that Kings, Archbishops and Ministers of State flung themselves in vain against them. So marvellously has the country advanced in wealth and intelligence, we venture to think that if Johnson could make another journey in the Hebrides, even his strong Tory and Episcopal prejudices would yield to the conviction that the Puritanism which has made modern Scotland, for we claim nothing less for it, though it may not suit all lands, has been an unmixed blessing there.

A far different state of things meets our view when we turn our eyes to Ireland. In recent years both countries have benefited by union with England, but while Scotland has become loyal, contented, intelligent, progressive, a kingdom at unity with itself, Ireland is torn with factions and—blatantly disloyal in three provinces; thrifty, " dour," unwavering in loyalty, though often sorely tried, in the fourth—is in fact not one, but two kingdoms, differing in religion, in character and sentiment.

It is a strange fact that every popular historian who has ventured on the task of presenting the case of Ireland, from the reign of Henry the Eighth to our own times, finds an explanation of its discontent and restlessness in the appalling cruelties inflicted on the native population by their English rulers. They might go further back than to Henry; Dermot and Strongbow, and later King John's forces, were not over-nice in their methods. We cannot deny nor can we excuse those cruelties. They were dire and they were unprofitable; and of all those who took in hand the hard task of bending the Irish to the will of England, and forcing them to accept the Protestant faith, Cromwell's hand was heaviest and hardest. The massacre of the Drogheda garrison, even though the majority in it were English, was the most terrible act ever perpetrated by England on Irish soil. It leaves a stain on the great name of the Protector which time can never obliterate. In vain do his defenders plead in extenuation the ruthless reprisals of the Irish on the English colonists, and the memory of the butchery of 1641. To compare a man of Cromwell's intelligence and piety with an illiterate

Irish peasant, dispossessed of his home to make room
for a hated stranger, and burning with a sense of
wrong, is an absurdity too great for any just mind
to entertain.   If Cromwell wished to make Puritanism and his own name obnoxious to Irish Roman
Catholics he could hardly have chosen a more
certain method to accomplish his end. " The
curse of Cromwell on you," has been for long, and
may be still, one of the most fearful imprecations
one Irish peasant can pronounce on another. Not
by such means as the Protector employed is the
cause of true religion advanced. It is quite possible
that if all Ireland had embraced the Puritan form
of Christianity, its inhabitants might to-day be as
contented and loyal as the inhabitants of Scotland,
and the country the happiest and most prosperous
of the British Isles ; for though Puritanism has
failed utterly in the southern provinces, and left a
legacy of political and religious hatred, south
against north, and north against south, the northern
province is, as we have pointed out, cordially
attached to England, united, intelligent and prosperous.   Indeed, some are found bold enough to
assert that in no part of the British Empire is the
feeling of loyalty to the English Crown stronger
than in the province of Ulster, a feeling which pre-
vails also amongst the Protestants dwelling in the
other provinces.

The question, however, that is here under consideration, is whether or no the present condition
of Ireland may be attributed, in whole or in part,
to England's attempt—we must say England, for
Cromwell was not the only oppressor—to force

Protestantism on the country ? Again, can we
entertain the opinion, or is it a vain superstition,
that the inter-marriage of the Protestant settlers
with the Irish peasants, resulting in the bringing-up
of their offspring in the Roman Catholic religion
and in bitter opposition to English rule, was a judgment on England for its injustice ?

The answer to the former question, the latter we
decline, surely must be that while Puritanism—
for we may confine our answer to the effects of
that movement—has made a deep impression,
religious and political, though in totally different
manner, on Ireland, north and south, the main
causes of Irish unrest and discontent must be
sought for elsewhere. The Celt is not usually a
successful ruler. His temperament is against him.
He is of that race " which shakes all nations and
founds none." He has charm and ability ; but
he is passionate, explosive, volatile. He has a long
memory for injuries and a short one for benefits.
Cromwell is remembered while Swift is forgotten.
Puritanism, as has been suggested, might have
cured some of those faults, braced up the people,
and made them industrious, progressive, and self-
reliant, in far greater measure than they have ever
yet been ; but the country as a whole has, for good
or ill, rejected Puritanism, and England has not
only acquiesed in the rejection, but has betrayed
and hastened the downfall of the Protestant
garrison which it planted there.

Between the rival faiths it is not our business
here to judge, but if the England of Elizabeth and
of Cromwell honestly believed that a faith resting

on the Scriptures was better than a faith resting on
the Bishop of Rome, England ought to have adopted
Scriptural methods in its propagation. The peasantry ought to have had the Scriptures in their own
tongue, and pastors after their own hearts ; schools
and teachers, speaking both Irish and English,
would seem to have been a more sure and reasonable way of winning a wild and wayward people
than pikes and muskets ; and once a policy of enlightenment had been taken in hand it ought to
have been persevered in. But England faltered
and compromised, and at last, professing to make
tardy reparation for past severities, set about
buying out and disbanding the Protestant garrison.
To this vacillation, then, together with the Celtic
temperament, much more than to the memory of
anything Cromwell did in Ireland, must we attribute
the political and religious divisions of the country.
Puritanism may be regarded as a factor, but only
a factor, in rearing up two nations on the same
soil. But it is a tenable proposition that the native
character being what it is, the presence of a strong
Puritan element in the country is now a pressing
necessity ; and that, therefore, to weaken it or
coerce it would be only to add one more wrong to
a land that has suffered much from the exigences
of English politics and parties.

In the midst of all these changes, disputations,
and persecutions ; Roman Catholics hustled under
Elizabeth, Charles and Cromwell ; Protestants
flying across the seas to New England to escape the
savagery of Tyrconnel and James ; the industries
of both parties ruined by the selfish policy of

English manufacturers ; it is pleasant to light on well-authenticated instances of the working of a more kindly spirit in both Irish parties. When the Roman Catholic population, in 1641, rose to exterminate the Protestant settlers, and during the later sufferings of the Protestants under Tyrconnel, many a poor Catholic peasant sheltered and succoured a Protestant neighbour at the risk of his own life ; on the other hand when the absurd and humiliating Penal Laws were enacted, against the will of a large number of intelligent Irish Protestants, the latter found a way of evading the laws by treating them as a dead letter over the greater part of the country.   How beautiful and how inexplicable is the working of the mind of " dark Rosaleen ! "

CHAPTER XI

IT is hardly necessary to offer proof of the influence
of the Puritan movement on the Protestant popu-
lations of the Continent. From the moment that
England was caught up in the cleansing storm of
the sixteenth century, a process of giving and
receiving began between this country and the
Reformed Churches abroad. Little as our sympathies may be now with the findings of the Synod
of Dort, that assembly, attended as it was by
English divines, affords an illustration of the working of this process. To the mind that is not by
nature reactionary, or cramped with insularity,
the benefit of such mutual intercourse will be at
once acknowledged. When Europe was in the
throes of the Reformation, there was not a town in
Europe, whose inhabitants were struggling for
religious and political freedom, that did not look
to England as the champion of liberty. And when
at a later period half Europe was wrenched from
the movement, and, but for the valour of Gustavus
Adolphus, all might have been lost, England was
still the hope of the awakened peoples abroad.
Under the Stuart dynasty the succour they received was scanty, and for the most part rested on

policy; but in the days of the Protector it was
wholehearted and sincere; and, whether sympathy
with their friends or personal taste be the explanation, it is a fact that if we were to visit any of the
Reformed Churches abroad, now in this twentieth
century, and witness their worship on a Sunday
morning, we should find, in France, Switzerland,
Holland, Italy, or in the lately-formed Spanish and
Portuguese Churches, a form of worship resembling,
in almost every particular, the descriptions we
have had of Sabbath mornings in early Puritan
times.

A visit to our English colonies, Canada and
Australia, would often yield a similar result.
Colonial Protestantism is strongly Puritan, both
in its religious sentiment and its political ideals.
Indeed, we have it, on the authority of those best
able to judge,[1] that the Puritan presentation of
Christianity, whether by an Episcopal or non-
Episcopal Church, or by both, most readily wins
acceptance in our colonies, with all the inhabitants,
excepting of course, those of the Roman Catholic
faith.   On the other hand, like the Unionists of
Ulster, they have a high appreciation of, and even
an affectionate attachment to, the English Crown.
In this latter circumstance they present a contrast
to the French Protestants, whose devotion to the
Republic amounts to a passion, and whose detes-
tation of some of the former rulers of their country remains unsubdued by time.

The influence of French Protestants in the Army
and the Senate and the Law Courts, is, in its

---

[1] Colonial and Continental Church Society.

importance, out of all proportion to their number in the nation ; and if, as we believe, France has been much affected by English Puritanism we have here proof of the continuance of its influence. In lesser degree this may be said of Italy, for every effort made in that country, towards securing a simpler form of worship and a more evangelical expression of faith, receives substantial support from the Puritan party in England ; and the patriotic party in Italy have never forgotten, and probably never will forget, that when Garibaldi struck for a united Italy, the Puritans in England stood solidly at his back and welcomed him with rapturous rejoicings when he landed on our shores.

This side glance at the Continent of Europe, while giving us the assurance that Puritanism is still a living, and, at all events politically, a growing force, may prepare us for a brief sketch of its influence on the great English-speaking Republic of America. Puritanism made America ; and a glance at the names of its presidents—the free choice of a free people—from Lincoln's day to Wilson's, gives an indication of the spirit which still rules that country. With scarcely an exception they have been men into whom the religious and political ideals of the men of the " Mayflower" —without their intolerance and narrowness—had entered freely and largely. It was in reference to the early English settlers in Virginia and Massachusetts an American Admiral recently made the witty remark, " It was a fine old hen that hatched the American eagle."

It is important to bear in mind that in the colon-

ising of America there were at least three stages.
The first stage was what was known as Raleigh's
settlement in Virginia, a very mixed company of
adventurers, yet possessing the natural doggedness
and endurance of the race which enabled them to
bear up against hardships and sufferings such as
have rarely been met with. These heroic souls,
numbering one hundred and five, left England in
1607, and crossed the stormy Atlantic in three
small vessels, no larger than fishing boats. Several
died of cold and exposure on the voyage; the
remainder narrowly escaped shipwreck and on
reaching land had scarcely strength to disembark.
They were houseless and lacked almost every
necessary of life; the native Indians were sus-
picious and unfriendly; and were it not for aid
from the Mother Country, in clothing and food and
farming utensils, generously supplied by friends,
they must all have famished. " *Tantae molis erat
Romanam condere gentem.*" An American writer
has truly observed that " this first English settlement would probably have been the last, if the
English colonists had not been so strong and
courageous." A third stage was that of the Roman
Catholic settlers in Maryland in 1634, of whom
little has been written, but who appear to have been
a very peaceful and tolerant company. They had
left England because of the laws against recusants,
and it being impossible to found a purely Roman
Catholic colony, they chose the nobler part, and
proclaimed general religious liberty. All these are,
however, overshadowed by the romantic story of
the men of the " Mayflower," that little bark of one

hundred and eighty tons burden, which sailed from
Southampton in 1620, with its human freight of
forty-one male passengers and their families.
This group of settlers had first fled to Holland to
escape the persecutions to which the Sectaries were
subjected in England. Truth compels us to admit
that many of them were difficult to reason with.
If they received hard blows they were ready to
return them, and indeed their English sympathisers,
when times changed, did return them in many
instances with interest; and their treatment of
their fellow Christians in the new land forms a very
dark chapter in their history, and compares un-
favourably with the generous policy of the Maryland settlers of 1634. "No person within this
province," ran the first law of this Roman Catholic
settlement, "professing to believe in Jesus Christ
shall be in any ways troubled, molested, or dis-
countenanced for his or her religion, or in the free
exercise thereof." With far different feelings, than
those which possess us, would we now think upon
the founders of the Plymouth colony if they
had displayed a like reasonable and conciliatory
spirit.

Yet with all their failings they formed a noble
company and made great sacrifices for conscience
sake. They loved England, and it was sorely
against their inclination they left it; but to
remain there was, in their judgment, to suffer the
worst bondage man can be made subject to, the
bondage of the mind. Little they knew of the
hardships which awaited them when they started
on that memorable voyage, notwithstanding the

H

tidings which had reached them from Virginia from time to time.

But once on American soil they were free. Free to live their own life, make their own laws, and most important of all to their minds, free to worship God according to their conscience.

The English colonies numbered thirteen in all, of which Georgia was the last, founded in 1733; but the three emigrations mentioned here must be regarded as the vital steps in colonisation.

As with England so it has been with America, every European country has sent its emigrants thither; but to those English settlers of the seventeenth century belongs the glory of founding the western Republic. As years passed the narrowness of the early Puritans passed with them, but their higher endowments remained. Gradually the settlements consolidated, with Jamestown as the seat of the first national assembly; fresh Puritan emigrants poured into Massachusetts; over seventeen hundred landing in a few years; and amongst those later comers were men of the best blood in England, landed gentry, scholars from Oxford and Cambridge, learned divines, lawyers, shrewd men of business, and, best of all for a new country, God-fearing Puritan farmers from Lincolnshire and the eastern counties. "These men," writes Green "were driven from their fatherland not by earthly want, or greed of gold, or by lust of adventure, but by the fear of God, and the zeal for a godly worship."

Language must quite fail in any attempt to

compare America of to-day, still fresh and young, with the America on whose shores these first one hundred and five settlers landed, a little more than three hundred years ago. The land was then a wilderness of prairie, mountain, desert and plain, seventy-five times larger than England, inhabited by Indians and extending nearly three thousand miles from the Atlantic to the Pacific. The America of our day is indeed a country of many peoples, to the number of about one hundred millions, and of many faiths ; but in language, laws, literature, civilisation and even religion, it has stamped upon it the deep impression of our Puritan forefathers. " The immigration from England and Scotland," says a writer in Chambers' Encyclopaedia, " has mainly fixed the type of civilisation alike in the United States and in Canada." There can be little doubt that the constitution of America—though it would have been more to the mind of Vane than of Pym and Hampden—would have proved acceptable to all the really practical politicians of the Puritan party. The somewhat despotic powers with which the President is invested, far exceeding those of an English monarch, might present an obstacle ; but, on the other hand, the large liberty enjoyed by the separate States would almost certainly redress the balance in their minds.

We can well believe also that the religious atmosphere of the United States would be found by such spirits as Milton and Baxter entirely satisfactory. The religious freedom for which those great souls yearned, flourishes there ; the fairest flower of the nation ; while the publication of the Scriptures, the evangelising of Jew and Heathen, the planting of the Hebrew race as a nation in Palestine—all dear to the heart of the Protector and to the more enlightened men of his time—are works and movements which never fail of generous support and eloquent advocacy. A successful work of evangelisation in Korea is in American hands, and has already resulted in the baptism of over a hundred thousand natives. The Student Volunteer movement, which aims at winning the world to Christianity, and has its branches in America, Canada, Europe and Asia, is led by an American citizen of great ability and deep piety. With such facts facing us, as we contemplate the political and religious position of modern America, who will say that Puritanism is dead ? As these facts prove, it lives as a permanent influence in the laws and the Christianity of the Republic.

The same might be said of American literature. America has had no Shakespeare or Milton, no philosophers, like Bacon and Berkeley, no political genius like Hobbes and Edmund Burke ; nevertheless, in all these departments of knowledge, it maintains a high level of excellence, and a moral tone worthy of the best Puritan traditions. The deep outpourings of Walt Whitman, and the triflings of Mark Twain, may leave quiet, serious-minded English folk unmoved ; but Longfellow and Whittier, and even the unhappy Poe— " oscillating between the gutter and the skies,"

yet whose poems are restrained and chaste—
if not poets of the first rank, touch deep feelings
and raise our thoughts above the fleeting things
of time and sense ; while prose writers like Emer-
son and Washington Irving, and novelists, like
Hawthorne, will continue to be as highly ap-
preciated in England as in their own country
for many generations, taking their place amongst
our own standard works of literature.

If we harbour a fear for America, strangely
enough it is caused by the same element, and
springs from the same source which has made,
both England and America great, generous,
religious, chivalrous. We have spoken of the
thrift of the Puritans and of the great expansion
of English trade resulting from it. In the later
history of the movement it will be found that
the love of riches, and an absorbing interest in
trade, to a large extent, cooled the passion for
religion felt by the first generation of " Professors,"
and produced a Laodicean temper amongst its
followers, which spread through the length and
breadth of the land, so that throughout the greater
part of the Hanoverian period religion had touched
low-water mark. This is the real danger to the
higher life of America. It may be tempted to
barter moral greatness for material. But we
will not give way to despondency, knowing that,
humanly speaking, the future of the world rests
with the two great Puritan nations, England and
America. Acting together, and acting in righteousness, the world is safe. Let us, therefore,
cherish the hope for our English-speaking brethren

across the Atlantic, (as for ourselves), that the Puritanism which nurtured their childhood, and in somewhat altered outward form, attended their riper years, and impressed itself indelibly on their laws, their literature and their religion, will not fail them when their country reaches old age. In this connection we may give Professor Farrand's judgment, who will have it that the pursuit of gain did more for religion than the churches :—" Conservative church-goers were shocked by the unorthodox and godless behaviour of the people, whereas the liberally inclined insisted that they were displaying a more genuine and therefore a more deeply religious spirit. It was a world-old difference, but the turn which it took was indicative of the time as well as of American conditions. If New England was not the leader it was typical of the rest of the country, and there the old religious ideals were taking on more of an ethical cast, they were becoming more practical, and men were turning in the direction of philanthropy and social reform."[1] This judgment of Professor Farrand's may be supplemented by that of Lord Morley. In a passage of rare eloquence, in his Recollections, we have as just an appreciation of America's commercial magnates as has ever been inscribed. "Private munificence moved by the spirit of high public duty has never been shown in a finer scale than by American plutocracy working in a democratic atmosphere. Materialist, practical,

---

[1] Farrand, " Development of the United States," p. 130.

and matter of fact as the world of America may
be judged, or may perhaps rightly judge itself,
everybody recognises that commingled with all
that is a strange elasticity, a pliancy, an intellectual subtlety, a ready excitability of response
to high ideals, that older worlds do not surpass,
even if they can be said to have equalled them."[1]
    A final word has to be said about America, to
which England in those days contributed every
type of religionist existing within its own borders;
Romanists to Maryland; sympathisers with
prelacy to Virginia; Puritanism of many variants
to New England. Amongst those variants we
class Quakerism, for we hold Morley[2] to be right
when he alleges —thus differing from Church of
England historians—that "Puritanism in its
turn threw out an extreme left with a hundred
branches of its own." One of those branches,
unquestionably, was George Fox's 'Society of
Friends'; persecuted at home, "many took
refuge in America to be even more severely persecuted by their Puritan friends in New England.
Penn, son of the famous Admiral, obtained a
charter from Charles the Second to found the
colony of Pennsylvania, where his much tried
co-religionists at last found rest. Whatever
view we may take of the tenets of this remarkable
sect, they alone, of all the English colonists,
exhibited, in the political principles with which
they governed the state, "the sweet reasonableness" of the Founder of Christianity. What

---

[1] Vol. II. p. 109.   " Cromwell," p. 44.

Maryland promised, and in part fulfilled, they
granted in fullest measure. They alone treated
the unfortunate natives, despised alike by
Romanists and New Englanders, as fellow-
creatures, possessing equal rights with white
men, and entitled to just payment for any land
of theirs the white man occupied, and while
tolerating slavery these Quaker settlers hated it,
and aimed at its suppression.[1] To this goodly
company must be added the Anglo-Scots,
planted by England in Ulster, and then ruined
by their creator by a long series of commercial
laws, directed to the protection of English manufacturers. These colonists, chiefly Scotch by
nationality and Presbyterian by religion, under
pressure of this tyranny left Ulster in great
numbers for America. We read of the men of
the "Mayflower" gazing with tearful eyes on the
shores of their native land, as they faded from
their view, and with heavy hearts exclaiming
"farewell, dear England," but we may rest
assured no such feelings possessed the breasts of
our Scotch friends, who felt they had had quite
enough of England and its political tergiver-
sations and inconstancy. It is not surprising
that out of those various elements, in process of
time, there was evolved a solid democracy,
determined on working out its own political
salvation in its own way.

Reference has been made to the consolidation
of this group of British settlements, but it was
a consolidation rather due to the nature of things

---

[1] Journal of John Woolman, p. 145.

than to design, accidental rather than premeditated. "In all the colonies," writes Chesterton, "the Government was substantially the same. It was founded in every case upon Charters granted at some time or other to planters by the English King. In every case there was a Governor who was assisted by some sort of elective assembly. The legislature was in some form or other elected by free citizens." Here then we have, if not the name, the substance of democracy. The principle was rooting itself in the new world, from the simple fact that it was rooted in the hearts of those Puritan settlers, and in time became acceptable to Virginia and Maryland. This "is explicable," says Chesterton,[1] "only when we remember that to the unspoiled conscience of man as man, democracy will ever be the most self-evident of truths. It is the complexity of our civilisation that blinds us to its self-evidence, teaching us to acquiesce in irrational privilege as inevitable, and at last to see nothing strange in being ruled by a class, whether of nobles or of Parliamentarians. But the man who looks at the world with the terrible eyes of his first innocence, can never see an unequal law as anything but an iniquity, or Government divorced from the general will as anything but usurpation," This may be quite true, but reflection will show us that such sentiments are deserving of currency only in a perfect state and amongst men who are perfect. We are far

---

[1] "History of the United States," p. 13.

from this at present, and it is to be feared that Chesterton's views have in them all those elements of anarchy which prudent minds discovered in the writings of Milton. Democracy which is, we have maintained, a dominant note of Puritanism needs the predominant Puritan note of righteousness to make it safe. England and America, the two most genuinely democratic nations in the world, could never have become what they are had not Puritanism given them along with its political ideals that Godliness which was the very life of its life. So long as such principles are living and active we can trust the general will, but once divorce them we must fall back on despotism as the only means of preserving peace and order. "For I say at the core of democracy, finally is the religious element. All the religions new and old are there. Nor may the scheme step forth clothed in resplendent beauty and command, till these bearing the best, the latest fruit, the spiritual, shall fully appear."[1]

It is quite possible that as the American colonies grew in wealth and numbers they would, had no quarrel arisen, one day have quietly slipped their moorings with the old country and claimed independence. The failure on England's part to discern the essentially democratic spirit of the new world made separation inevitable. The children of men who preferred exile to coercion, were not going to submit to coercion in a land which their own labour had turned from a

---

[1] Walt Whitman, "Democratic Vistas."

prairie to fertile fields and peaceful homes. All that was needed to effect and accelerate the revolution was a stubborn monarch without imagination and without foresight; and we got him in the third of the Georges; an estimable person if he had not the misfortune to be born a king. The Stamp Act, and "The Boston Tea Party," may be passed over here with the remark that, without the impositions connected with these incidents, the colonies could not be held unless English ministers understood the mind of the colonists and respected their liberties. If we wished to retain them, it had been wisest to trust them and leave them alone. When Grenville, it was said, began to read American dispatches the colonies were lost. At the same time throughout the war of Independence, there was no feeling of hatred to the Mother Country: in fact as is the case in most wars, a large number never understood the cause of the disagreement or what they were fighting for, the motives which led them to offer their services being of a very mixed character. Professor Farrand of Yale has thought it worth while to recall the gossip of those times, which attributed the revolt, not to the Tea Tax, but to the girls of Boston who were showing a decided preference for English young men and a rather saucy disparagement of Americans. "What brought me in," said one young Bostonian, "was not the tax but that a red-coat English gallant stole my sweetheart from me." [1]   Well, "*spreteaque injuria formae*"

---

[1] Max Farrand, "Development of the United States," p. 36.

is a very old ground of complaint, and we give
it here for what it is worth ; at the same time
retaining the opinion that the root cause of the
trouble was the failure of George and his Ministers
to recognise that the political principles of the
Puritans had been more or less accepted by all
the States, and that such principles were hostile
to any legislation that was not supported by the
express will of the people affected by it.

CHAPTER XII

THE political history of England during the greater part of the nineteenth century is interwoven with its trade. The interests of commerce and manufacture, of railroads and shipping, of exports and imports, occupied a large amount of public attention, while the struggle between the land party and the rising industrial party was fought out in the House of Commons, resulting in an extended franchise and a lop-sided form of Free Trade, and the dominance for many years of what is known as the Manchester School. It is not surprising that men of culture were troubled at the sordidness of the age and felt constrained to protest against it. There is something of petulance in Tennyson's outburst " we are not cotton spinners all," but at the time it was excusable ; for in truth the cotton spinners, with their one-sided Free Trade and their peace hobbies, would have left us with a mere skeleton army, a miserably attenuated navy, and a little England, possessing no adequate defences, and consequently, counting for nothing in the councils of the nations of Europe. Free Trade is much to be desired, but it is a doubtful benefit when it is all on one side ; and we would all of us fain beat our swords into ploughshares were it not that across the narrow sea our neighbour is sharpening his in order to cut our throats. This little England policy, though advocated by men who would doubtless claim to be the successors of the seventeenth century Puritans, was far removed from the policy of the Protector, who would see his country not only prosperous at home, but capable of defending itself abroad, and influencing the policy of other countries, through the knowledge that it was strong on sea and land. Nor can we attribute the peace policy wholly to a more enlightened national conscience than that of the earlier period ; for, indeed, it is too true that along with a profession of religion of a somewhat sombre Puritanical type, there was often found a callous disregard of the comforts and just claims of the working classes. The hours of labour were long, the remuneration small, many of the homes void of comfort and cheerfulness, schools insufficient and recreations hardly existent. Under conditions such as these enormous fortunes were built up by men of the capitalist class, many of whom posed in Parliament as friends of the people, while opposing reforms which might have made their lot lighter, and appeared before the public as munificent philanthropists, heading subscription lists with large donations which they could easily spare, and which might have been more worthily spent, without ostentation, in paying higher wages to their workers and providing them with happier homes. There were, of course, many bright exceptions to this policy

amongst the employers ; men who not only carried
on their business in a spirit of justice, but
also took a humane interest in the lives of the
operatives and their families. The praise accorded
to the conduct of employers of this class is, however,
the strongest proof of its exceptional character.
Had it been general it would have been taken as
a matter of course, and a pleasing illustration of
the happy relation existing between the two
classes. We may charitably hope that the very
dependent condition of the workers, with the
dread of unemployment and hunger ever present,
was due in general to want of thought rather
than to complete indifference to their happiness
on the part of the masters. Labour was regarded
as an article to be bought and sold ; only amongst
the more thoughtful and conscientious employers
did the thought of a common brotherhood of
men prevail. The question " Am I my brother's
keeper ? " if asked at all, was asked only to be
dismissed ; when the labourer had received the
penny a day agreed upon, the matter came to an
end.

It may justly be said that the whole of this
commercial situation, good and bad, both as
regards the increase of wealth and power, and
the unfavourable state of the ordinary hand,
was the creation of the Puritan. His thrift,
industry, shrewdness and general uprightness
made him a first rate man of business ; while
the cheapness of the labour market and the long
hours of labour enabled him to secure the foremost place in the markets of the world. But it

will at once be seen that if Puritanism was to
maintain its position as a religious force, working
for righteousness, the situation which it had
created must be altered in the interests of
the dependent worker. While the plea that
want of thought on the part of English manufacturers accounts for many of the hardships
of the workers, when we recall the unfriendly
attitude of the former to the landed gentry, an
attitude somewhat tinged with malice, we may
feel inclined to modify our charitable judgment.

The facts, fairly examined and stated, do not
bear out the charges made against the great
English landlords by some popular political
writers. Poverty, disease, insanitary dwellings
could be found in many places ; but let it be
remembered that principles of sanitation, and
hygienics in general, were little understood in
those days. The castles and manor houses of
the great, the Public Schools, the Colleges of
Oxford and Cambridge left much to be desired
in such matters; no wonder then if villages and
hamlets shared the common lot. But the case
as presented in Disraeli's "Sybil," and in Mrs.
Green's "Epilogue"[1] is misleading if taken as a fair
picture of England as a whole. Such simple
tales as "the Copsley Annals" and the "Memoirs
of Leigh Richmond" give a far juster and far
happier picture of England at the close of the
eighteenth and the early years of the nineteenth
century ; and what these accounts, drawn from
life, tell us of the labouring classes in Shropshire,

---

[1] Green's Short History, Ed. 1916.

Bedford, Sussex, must have been true of many
other counties as well. Landlords like " Lord
Marney "—hard, obstinate, unsympathetic, ex-
acting, selfish—existed beyond a doubt. They
were a dishonour to their order and their country ;
but on the other hand, squires like Lyttelton
Powys, might be found in hundreds up and
down the land, for one who represented the
Marney type. Powys and his neighbouring
squires, without abating any claims which they
considered, rightly or wrongly, belonged to their
position by an arrangement of Divine Providence,
foregathered with the Bedfordshire farmers,
labourers, and small shop-keepers, at harvest
homes and Friendly Society anniversaries,
treated them as men and brothers, looked after
their welfare and encouraged habits of thrift and
sobriety ; and, instead of squalor, disease and
misery, we see a picture of a smiling country-
side, a happy peasantry, a faithful pastor of the
best Puritan stamp, and a just landlord class.
Mr. Richmond, who was Rector of Turvey, founded
a Friendly Society in his parish with three
branches ; a children's club, a women's club and
a men's club, each class contributing according
to its means and receiving substantial aid in
times of sickness. No better proof can be given
of the value and popularity of these clubs than
the fact that almost the whole of the labouring
population of this parish joined them, which is
also evidence of the fairly prosperous condition
of the people. Poor, no doubt, they were, but

[1] " Memoirs of Leigh Richmond," p. 91.

I

far removed from actual want. The clubs were in a thoroughly solvent condition, since, in addition to the contributions of the beneficiary members, there were some twenty honorary members belonging to the much maligned landlord class.

It may be argued that Turvey was an exception; but any such statement is refuted by Mr. Grimshawe's account of the proceedings at the annual festivals, when several clergymen, some from near and some from distant parishes, were accustomed to attend as visitors, in order to compare the conduct of the Turvey clubs with those they had established in their own parishes.

One of the visitors, coming from a manufacturing district in the north, dwells pathetically on the miserable state of the women and children in his parish as compared with the happy and healthy population of the parish of Turvey.

Here then we find, as one of the most wholesome influences in the country, Puritan squires and Puritan clergy working together for the common good and working with success; and this at a time when Puritanism in the minds of many was as good as dead; as a matter of fact it dominated both religious and social life at this period in every well ordered parish in England.

To anyone who has a fair knowledge of the life of the average English squire, "they toil not, neither do they spin" is a cruel libel on his class, though received with applause when uttered by a popular demagogue, and quoted with satisfaction in a section of the Press. Has modern Radicalism forgotten that Hampden, Pym,

Hutchinson, St. John, Vane, Cromwell, and the Country Party which supported them, were all of the landed gentry class, and that they were the men who won for England her political and religious freedom ? To many it will be felt to have been an evil day for the country when the political party in the nineteenth century, which sympathised most with Puritan religion, began to attack real property and to lay heavy burdens on the land, burdens which have increased to such an extent that we are in danger of clearing the country-side of its most wholesome element. An impartial observer must surely judge that, if we are bent on preserving our Free Trade policy, it is essential that we should remove every possible burden from the land, unless we mean to ruin home agriculture. Land tax, tithe, and all such burdens, should be redeemed, so that the English farmer may have his land at a low rent and compete on equal terms with foreign imports. Recognising that in all essentials the majority of English landlords are as truly Puritan as the traders and manufacturers of the country, it was a most unfortunate circumstance that any root of bitterness was ever permitted to spring up and divide them. Had the two parties worked together for the common good, as they had worked in the days of Pym and Hampden, we should have found a country at all times united, contented, prosperous and strong, in the presence of any threatened danger from outside, and less susceptible to revolutionary tendencies within. But unhappily their paths diverged, and for many years each party seemed, to the unbiassed onlooker, to be engaged in a defence of its own interests and privileges and in attacking the interests and privileges of the other; land against trade, and trade against land. On the whole trade has had decidedly the best of it; and, if we substitute Labour for trade, we may say it is now the only privileged class in the community, while it has succeeded in imposing a burden on land so heavy and so unequal that it seems impossible, under the most favourable climatic conditions, to support it. It would be unfair to accuse leaders like Bright and Cobden, and the Puritan politicians who adopted their fiscal programme, of having aimed deliberately at the destruction of what is called landlordism, but their policy undoubtedly tended in that direction; while the obscurantism and obstinacy of many of the landed gentry helped to give momentum to such policy. At the same time we should now find ourselves thinking more kindly of the great Manchester School, had those who composed it shown a greater readiness to support the efforts which men like Lord Shaftesbury made, for the improvement of the lot of factory women and children, and less disposition to harass interests with which they were but imperfectly acquainted.

Bright and his party could have done much to lighten the lot of factory operatives without any legislation, but their action or inaction left them open to the suspicion that the landed interests and agriculture were sacrificed to the Manchester desire for cheap labour, which could not be had without cheap food, and cheap food meant the passing of the English cornfield. The Factory Act of 1878, one of the most valuable of many such acts, was hailed as a great concession to the workers in textile factories, but it left a working day of 12 hours length, with two hours for meals and a half-day on Saturdays. In workshops in which no children were employed, the hours for women were from 6 a.m. to 9 p.m. with $4\frac{1}{2}$ hours for meals and absence. In other factories children of ten years of age might be engaged. Where, under such conditions as these, we may ask, were the opportunities and time for self-improvement and recreation? And why was such legislation necessary at all? The capitalists on whom it was imposed ought to have anticipated it, or made it unnecessary by generous and humane regulations of their own, far exceeding anything this law demanded of them. It is however notorious that they failed to do so; and the situation was rendered somewhat amusing, if not actually comic, by the appearance of a sort of encyclical, from the pen of Mr. Bright to the farmers of England, in strong condemnation of the Game Laws.

Mr. Bright's letter on the Game Laws brought little comfort to the farmers, whose corn growing he had ruined, and we are not surprised that on the occasion of his visit to the West of England, a farmer approached him in the Red Lion Hotel at Truro, and shaking a menacing fist in his face greeted him with the uncomplimentary title " Ya owld rascal."

But if Bright could not see the incongruity of leaving to other hands the task of righting the wrongs of the cotton spinners, which was obviously his first duty, while he launched out in defence of the farming interest, of which he knew little, he was no conscious hypocrite. His disinterested conduct during the American Civil War of 1861, when to his own loss he took the side of the North, is worthy of all praise ; and his equally independent action when Home Rule for Ireland was proposed by his great leader, Gladstone, proved him, whether mistaken or not, to be a man of honour and conscientiousness. We shall describe in another chapter how relief and enlargement came, from another Puritan quarter, for the overworked and underpaid factory hands.

CHAPTER XIII

PLUTOCRAT AND PATRICIAN

HARROW-ON-THE-HILL is a fair place. It is one of
the three great schools which seem to the outsider to
be in a ringed fence, though for all their high pretensions they may be no better than their neighbours. For where is the dog that would dare move
a tongue against any of our Public Schools ? They
are all good, the very best, and it is part of an
Englishman's duty, may we not say of his religion,
to have an unwavering faith in them. In all
seriousness they have more than justified themselves as the builders of English character, in
manliness, truthfulness and patriotism. If men
become Sophists, and intellectually dishonest, in
later years, it is not through anything they carry
with them from our Public Schools, and nothing
seems less likely to improve or increase their moral
efficiency than certain recent proposals, in which
zeal outruns wisdom, to give them a "Catholic"
tone, and bring them under the sway of Ecclesiastics. Harrow is romantic. Its position gives
meaning to its name, and its name is poetic ; its
life links with the great Tudor Queen and with that
splendid rebel, Raleigh—courtier, soldier, hero,
adventurer, gallant English gentleman. 'Tis good,
on Speech days, to visit the school on the Hill and

hear five hundred lusty young English voices pro-
claiming, to all the listening earth, that "We began
when he began our times are one." We have
heard that the roar of Harrow, at Lord's, produces
pallor in the cheek and a trembling in the knees of
its great rival. Having heard the boys sing we are
not disposed to doubt it; but we are thankful it
has done something much more worthy of mention.
Somewhere about 1813, came to Harrow a youth of
twelve years, who, even at that tender age, had
found religion of the experimental stamp, dear to
the Puritan heart. "My minister tells me," said
Professor Blackie of Edinburgh, "that I have all
the virtues except a sense of sin." Where the
Professor failed this young Harrovian excelled.
A sense of sin, his own and men's in general, filled
his young heart, troubled his mind; yet not
troubled it to the point of despair, for had not the
faithful Maria Millis, a trusted domestic of his rather
worldly home, from whom he received his earliest
and deepest religious impressions, taught him the
meaning of the three R's—Ruin, Redemption,
Regeneration? On that foundation his religious
life rested, and it was never disturbed. When in
after years his cousin Pusey admonished him,
suggesting that he wholly misunderstood the views
of the Tractarians, he, nothing daunted, retorted
"Are you quite sure, dear cousin, you understand
them yourself?" When Seeley's alarming book,
"Ecce Homo," made its appearance he denounced
it as the wickedest thing that "had ever been
vomited from the jaws of hell." Maria Millis would
have said the same, and so, possibly, would Baxter.

Here we see the Puritan, jealous of any questioning of the crown rights of Christ, refusing to make terms with anyone who would remove a single landmark of the Evangelical Faith. Yet for all this Puritan rigidity, as it will appear to some, he did not despise carnal learning. If his old nurse had given him conscientiousness and industry, his school gave him a sufficient knowledge of letters to win him a first class in classical honours at Oxford.

Outside the old Speech Room of Harrow, on a wall that impinges on the road, may be seen a metal tablet which announces that at that spot Lord Ashley, when a boy at Harrow School, stood and saw a pauper's funeral ; a body carried to burial by four drunken men, shouting, cursing, wrangling as they staggered along.[1] The feelings of horror and pity which this spectacle aroused in him led him from that moment to consecrate his life to the well-being of the poor ; and right nobly the resolve was carried out. When the day came for him to take his place in Parliament he soon found himself confronted by an unexpected hostility on the part of Puritan nonconformity. Though himself a Puritan in doctrine he shared, with many of his class, a not altogether groundless suspicion that the Nonconformist in business did not always square with the Nonconformist at the prayer meeting. More than this he had, up to the time of his becoming acquainted with the writings of Philip Doddridge, a strong personal dislike of Dissenters ; but as he thinks of such a man as Doddridge, standing by the side of the infamous Pope

---

[1] Life of the Earl of Shaftesbury, Vol. I., Chap. 2.

Alexander the Sixth, before the Judge of all the earth, his feeling towards dissent softens. For the Dissenter there were the fields of Elysium. Alexander would go to his own place. But now he meets face to face men of whom he wished to think well, holding on steadfastly to the privileges of their class, privileges which he regarded as flagrantly unjust, robbing the poor of their wage, their health, and their morals.

Something no doubt had been done before this time to lighten the lot of the worker in factory and mine, but Acts of Parliament and good advice were evaded by the employers. A system of practical slavery existed in industrial England, and managers urged in defence of the system that thus only could the country defy the foreigner and keep its place in the world. We read of floggings, of bodies distorted by overwork, of women chained like beasts of burden to carts which they dragged through long underground galleries, covering in their journeys, to and fro, from seventeen to thirty miles a day. Children of tender age worked from 6 a.m. to 7 p.m., after which they went to school. If the small farmer and the agricultural labourer in a parish like Turvey, toiled long and made little, their lot was bliss compared with that of women and children working in the mines and factories. It would be untrue and unjust to say that all the capitalist class felt satisfied with this state of things ; the majority, and it was a large majority, belonged, both by social position and religious conviction, to the ranks of Nonconformist Puritanism. Many of them preached on Sundays, conducted Bible Classes

and prayer meetings and superintended Sunday
schools. Growing in wealth themselves they would
gladly see their workers healthy and satisfied.
But the concessions they were willing to make were
small, and they strongly resented anything like
drastic reform. At this point Greek met Greek;
the aristocratic Puritan faced the Puritan manufacturer and mine owner and a long fight began,
which continues to this day, under much changed
circumstances and with new combatants on either
side. When Lord Ashley entered Parliament
(1826), a few, but only a few, of the worst abuses in
the mines had been already dealt with. Humane
men of all creeds and political opinions had joined
in demanding legislation to lessen the sufferings of
the workers; but much remained to be done, and
here was the man to do it. He had the strong will
of his gifted ancestor, of ill repute, and brought to
the task what that ancestor neither possessed or understood, clean hands and a pure heart. It is little
to the credit of the National Church, at this time
represented chiefly by High-Churchmen of the
safe type, and a considerable Low Church party,
ignorantly confounded with the Evangelicals whom
it persecuted, that it did nothing as a corporate
body to raise the standard of life amongst the poor,
and to secure for them a just share of the result of
their labours. Individual parsons and squires and
mill-owners did something, in a sporadic way, but
it was as the light of a candle in the deep darkness.
The Clapham Sect, true friends of the poor, was for
the time busy over the slavery question, and
Kingsley, Maurice, and the " live " Broad Church-

men, as distinguished from the mere Platonists, had not yet arrived on the scene. The bishops were almost silent, and the average vicar was on the side of wealth and blue blood. He dined, as in Sir Roger's day, with the squire and was willing to preach Dr. South and the Bishop of St. Asaph on Sunday. Practically then, Ashley stood alone, facing the united forces of wealth, commercial knowledge and ability, and political power. Men, who were held in high repute as members of Christian churches or denominations, denounced, as tending to the destruction of trade, proposals for Parliamentary interference on behalf of the workers.

Bright, the tribune of the people, so ready to attack the sins of the landed class through Parliament, was intolerant when Parliament was invited to deal with the sins of his own class. He threatened to turn the key on his mills and throw on the legislators the responsibility of " feeding the millions whom they will not allow us to employ with a profit." Cobden would leave the helpless workers to make their own bargains, which meant no redress of their condition. Pease of Darlington proposed to close his factory if the labour of young persons was shortened to fifty-eight hours in the week, which works out, for child labour, an eleven hours day for five days and a short three hours day on Saturday. The aristocracy looked on, but gave Ashley no help. The clergy, and for a time, even the Evangelical church party, stood aloof, cowed by capital and power. Sir Robert Peel put every possible obstacle in the way ; some cabinet ministers scoffed at what they called " a Jack Cade

legislation "; Gladstone, who was at the Board of
Trade, never attempted to keep the House together
for Ashley, never gave him a vote or spoke a word
in his support. Yet in the darkest days, conscious
of the righteousness of his cause, and may we not
say of the righteousness of the English mind—in
the long run even of the minds of his opponents—
he neither expressed nor felt despair. Here was an
aristocrat to his finger tips, a Puritan of Puritans,
a man of culture and delicate taste, haughty and
somewhat austere amongst his equals, but whose
whole heart ran out to little chimney sweeps and
infant life toiling underground. For them ease,
power, social ties, a place in the Cabinet, were freely
sacrificed. " Should I deceive them," he writes,
" they will never henceforward believe that there
exists a single man of station or fortune who is
worthy to be trusted."[1] The result of Shaftesbury's (as we now name him) long struggle was
only a partial redemption of the poor ; but it broke
the ranks of his opponents and opened a way for
great reforms to follow. Twenty-two years of
labour on behalf of lunatics—whose treatment,
chained, starved, beaten, was an outrage on human
nature and a disgrace to Christianity—only procured a very imperfect lunacy Bill ; and twenty
years after the first effective Factory Act we find
him still pleading for upwards of two million oper-
ators who derived no benefit from it. But the
education of the wealthy and leisured classes had
begun, and the day was not far distant when every
respectable Englishman would be a " humanity-

---

[1] J. R. Green, " Short History," Epilogue, p. 864.

monger." We cannot boast that all social wrongs
have been removed ; indeed, as is often the case,
where reforms are on foot, in curing one set of ills
we created others equally serious. It is a painful
fact that the classes whose condition has been most
improved are developing a selfish, predatory
instinct, which is inflicting much hardship upon
other workers, and most of all upon the gentle
middle class, a class which is possessed of no political
influence and is not disposed to complain, but
which throughout the long history of the nation,
and under every form of Government, has been
more than any other, a power for righteousness.
This, however, is not a point to labour in these
sketches, as their main object is to illustrate Puritanism at work in Church and State ; and these
few pages, so far as they are true to facts, present
us with a picture of a Puritan aristocrat, who, by
the sheer force of his will and his deep piety, succeeded in changing the attitude of the House of
Commons and the Churches of England, towards
industrial occupations. England is still Puritan
to its heart's core, and the England of our day,
where it is touched by a genuine feeling of religion,
is merciful, tender, compassionate, just. Shaftesbury, and men like him, were the real prophets of
their day. It was not in our Cathedrals, our Taber-
nacles, our little Bethels, the most effective sermons
of the nineteenth century were preached, but from
the benches of the House of Commons. From
that great assembly words rang out which were
heard all over the land, and touched responsive
chords in a million hearts ; and their effect is seen

in the conversion of almost the whole of the successors of that party which opposed Shaftesbury, in
1826 and onwards, to the principles which he advocated. There was, as this account shows, much
alloy in the Puritanism of that period, and there is
much alloy in it still; but on the whole it is now
sweeter, juster, more lovable, more reasonable.
For the part Shaftesbury bore in producing this
change he deserves to be had in lasting remem-
brance; nor can we in this connexion forget the
faithful Puritan friend of his childhood, who taught
him his first prayer and drew his infant heart
heavenward. In the eyes of the great and just
Judge of mankind, perhaps Anthony Ashley Cooper
stands some-way below the humble, God-fearing,
Maria Millis.

CHAPTER XIV

BAXTER AND BUNYAN

It is hardly overstating facts to say that all that is best in English Christianity may be found in the writings of the two Puritan preachers whose names head this chapter; the message which they delivered to their country had been spoken by other voices, but its confirmation by Bunyan and Baxter has made it a message for all time, since England and America have set their names among the immortals; and so long as vital religion has place in these countries, so long will the Bedford tinker and the Kidderminster pastor continue to point the way to the Celestial City, and paint the joys of the Saint's Rest. We should, however, imagine a vain thing if we thought that men and women of the twentieth century can look on all or most of the problems of life and grace with the eyes of men and women of the seventeenth. "Bunyan's religious history," writes Professor Dowden, "recorded in his wonderful autobiography, may be repeated age after age in its essentials, for it is the history of a soul struggling from darkness to light, from confusion to clearness, from division to unity, from weakness to strength, from wretchedness to peace and joy; but if truths in the seventeenth century remain truths in the nineteenth, they operate under different conditions; they mingle with new elements in our minds; they require new adjustments; they must be translated into modern speech."[1] This may be taken as a fair statement of the whole Puritan position as it stands. As the child is father of the man, the Puritanism which struggled for freedom against Kings and Bishops, in the old times before us, is father of the Puritanism of our own day; the outward aspect differs, as the grown man from the child; knowledge grows, character takes shape, but personality remains, conscious of its past, and debtor to it willingly or unwillingly. It is impossible to treat Puritanism as something past and done with; something which arose a few hundred years ago, effected great changes in religion and politics and then, having served its day, disappeared to make room for some new force. The procedure of Parliament, the administration of law, the democratic spirit which rules our colonies, the American Republic, even the Salvationist, who sings with passionate earnestness at the street corner, "Come every soul by sin oppressed, there's mercy with the Lord," and not least, the spirit in which the two great Anglo-Saxon nations shouldered the burden and shared the awful sacrifices of the great war; all alike proclaim that Puritanism lives, not merely as an echo out of the past, but as something that can be seen

---

[1] Dowden, " Puritan and Anglican," p. 235.

K

and felt, possessed of a body with flesh and blood and bones, a soul to pity the oppressed and an arm to smite down tyranny.

Pym and Hampden still advocate ordered liberty; Oliver's Ironsides sing Psalms in dug-outs and pray as they go over the top; Sir Matthew Hale dispenses impartial justice and keeps the ermine clean; and Bunyan tenders solemn warning and spiritual counsel to the careless passer-by; and, unless England and America wholly renounce their past, "this shall be our portion for ever."

For this reason it is essential to our purpose to look at the rock from which we were hewn, as it may be seen in two of the most represent-ative characters of the period. But before doing so it may be well to enlarge for a moment on what has already been stated on the origins of Puritan-ism,[1] for the deeper the tree's roots, the wider the branches, and the greater must be its strength and powers of endurance. The Order of Francis-cans, founded in the early part of the thirteenth century, might be supposed to be far removed, in spirit and teaching, from the stern Protestant Sectaries of the seventeenth century, but Mr. Coulton, in his interesting mediæval studies, brings forward convincing proof that in their leading features the two movements closely resemble each other. Conversion, Assurance of Salvation, depravity of human nature, election, reprobation, meagreness of ritual, unadorned

---

See Chapter iii., p. 20.

Churches—plain as a Quaker Meeting House—
are all found amongst the followers of the gentle
St. Francis.[1] High Anglican writers, exasperated
by what they regarded as *La desolation des
Eglises*, in days of Puritan ascendancy, gave
expression to their sorrow in the words of the
Psalmist, " O God the heathen are come into
thine inheritance, thy holy temple have they
defiled. Thine enemies roar in the midst of thy
congregation. They break down the carved work
thereof (at once) with axes and hammers,"
yet all this could be matched, and even out-
matched, by the iconoclasm of the thirteenth
and fourteenth centuries. " Nor was that spirit
wanting," writes Coulton, " which thinks to do
God service by destroying objects of art which
the veneration of one party has rendered odious
to their religious adversaries." It is little understood that the pomps and magnificence of what
is known as Catholic worship were highly distasteful to the spirituals of St. Francis' day.
Images, painted windows, richly decorated build-
ings distracted the thoughts of worshippers ;
in fact some of the Friars preferred to worship in
mud Churches, and not until the fervour of
Evangelicalism, and even faith itself began to
decline, do we come to the miscalled age of Faith
which gave us most of the great Churches of the
middle ages. " The building of fine Churches
coincides exactly, not only in time but in logic,
with the persecution of these brethren who clung
strictly to the primitive Franciscan rule."[2] So

---

[1] First Series, p. 37.   [2] *Ibid.*

much for the Franciscans and their exhibition
both of the good and bad features of a later type
of Puritanism. About the middle of the fourteenth century there appeared upon the scene
in England another type of primitive Puritan,
bearing a name which some have interpreted as
meaning " a Psalm singer," others " a lazy
fellow." The Lollards drew their inspiration
and their theology from Wyclif's Bible, and
because of their intense devotion to it, basing all
life, conduct and doctrine on a bald literal
interpretation of its language, came soon to be
regarded as a dangerous element in the State.
Here we have an anticipation of the situation
created in a similar way by Ana-Baptists and
fifth-monarchy men some two hundred and
fifty years later. But Lollardism did something
far better than stir up political discontent
amongst English peasants. Wyclif's poor priests,
moving up and down the land, spread a knowledge of simple primitive Christianity amongst
the humbler classes to which they had been
strangers for many generations, and we recognise
in them the fore-runners of John Wesley's local
preachers, and indeed in the whole Lollard revival
a striking likeness to the Methodist revival of the
eighteenth century, which was a decidedly Puritan
movement from first to last. Some writers
entertain no doubt that the Lollards prepared
the soil for the peasant revolt of 1381 ; and it is
quite possible, for it is an almost invariable result
of the awakening of men's spiritual instincts
that they set themselves on the creation of a

more rational mode of temporal existence and a
sweeter atmosphere in which to enjoy it. Baxter
and his friends, and Cromwell most of all, were
insistent on the selection of good men for the
sacred ministry. Godly preachers, converted
men, men of blameless life ; that was the demand
of the Puritan. How closely this resembles the
Lollards' petition to Parliament in 1395, which
asks for the ordination of fit priests, the abolition
of clerical celibacy and vows of chastity ; and
protests against exorcism, the blessing of inanimate
objects, prayers for the dead, image worship,
pilgrimages, compulsory auricular confession, war
and capital punishment. In all this we see
points of contact with the seventeenth century
Sectaries, perhaps most of all with Quakers ;
and when we read of a rule that Lollards, known
by many as the " just-fast men," should marry
only among themselves, we are reminded of the
sadness which frequently took possession of a
Quaker Meeting, in the best days of that fraternity,
whenever one of its members proposed to marry
out of the Society. This high ancestry of Puritanism, to borrow the title of Mr. Coulton's essay,
and its reappearance time after time in the
religious and political history of the country, is
an almost certain guarantee of its permanency ;
but are we not justified in believing that, the
inwardness of the movement, the essential righteousness of the principles on which, and for which
it stood, is the best guarantee of all ? A glance
at some of these principles, as they are set forth
by one of the most noted prophets of the party—

divested of those unlovely accessories which were
never a necessary part of them, but rather a
hindrance to their progress—should confirm us
in this opinion. Richard Baxter was, perhaps,
the greatest of the Puritan divines and that is
saying much. He is also the most represent-
ative Puritan in history. The late Professor
Bigg has said " if you want to know what a
Puritan really was you cannot do better than
turn to the autobiographical sketch of Richard
Baxter." Baxter's " Self-Review " should, in
the opinion of Dean Stanley, be in the hands of
every student of theology, of every Minister of
Religion. " He there corrects the narrowness,
the sectarianism, the dogmatism of his youth
by the comprehensive wisdom acquired in long
years of persecution, of labour, and devotion."[1]
It is not possible here to give anything like a
sketch of this good man's life, but mention must
be made of certain stages in his career. Attracted,
Professor Bigg says, to religion by a book written
by the Jesuit Parsons, ordained in the Church
of England, he ends his life as a Nonconformist
minister. The explanation of his chequered life
is to be found in the circumstance that " some
zealous godly nonconformists " whom he met at
Shrewsbury, and whose fervent prayers and
savoury conference and holy lives he says " did
profit me much " were persecuted by the bishops ;
whereupon he found much prejudice arise in his
heart against the persecutors. The simple piety
of others, a rare thing in country places in those

---

[1] Introduction to Stanley's " Eastern Church."

days, made a deep impression on him and when
he found that they had no scruples against bishops,
and sought out and attended the ministry of
conformable clergy, who were Godly preachers,
and yet were despised as "Precisians, Puritans,
and Hypocrites, by the rest," he inclined the
more towards those new friends. The religious
laity in the country "were of the Evangelical
type, called by George Fox 'tender people,' a
quiet, old-fashioned race, who thought a great
deal about their souls and very little about vest-
ments or stone altars. Laud was worrying them
with fines and censures, wild curates were preaching what sounded to their simple ears like Roman-
ism, and the King was driving them into rebellion
by his forced loan."[1] We are not unfamiliar
with some of these causes of distress in our time,
and we do not wonder that Baxter and many
another pure soul found the Church no place for
them. Yet for all this we see Baxter, in his old
age, "weary of all this wordy strife, these notions,
forms and modes and names," finding all his
spiritual needs met in the Creed, the Lord's
Prayer and the Ten Commandments. "They
afford me now," he writes, "the most acceptable
and plentiful matter for all my meditations.
They are to me as my daily bread and drink."
In the autumn," he continues, "the life draws
down into the root, and so my mind may retire
to the root of Christian principles." It may
surprise some minds and comfort others to know
that this devout and scholarly Puritan conceived

---

[1] Bigg, "Wayside Sketches," quoted in "Self Review," p. x.

the possibility of a truly religious man, doubting
some parts of the Old Testament without abandoning the New; doubting even some parts
of the New Testament without abandoning the
fundamental principles of the Christian Faith
In 1671 he writes : " One instance I more doubt
of myself, which is when Christ and His Apostles
do oft use the Septuagint in their citations out of
the Old Testament, whether it be always their
meaning to justify each translation and particle
of sense as the Word of God rightly done; or
only to use that as tolerable, and containing the
main truth intended, which was then in use among
the Jews, and therefore understood by them;
and so best, as suited to the Auditors." Baxter
was Evangelical to the last degree, yet may he not
be aptly described as the father of the modern
devout broad Churchman ? He is, in his love
of truth, as Mark Pattison points out, essentially
Protestant ; he will have no traffic with falsehood
or make-belief. Truth must be followed at any
cost. " As long as you are uncertain," he says,
" profess yourself uncertain ; and if men condemn
you for your ignorance where you are willing to
know the truth, so will not God ; but when you
are certain, resolve in the strength of God, and
hold fast whatever it costs you, even to the death ;
and never fear being losers by God, by His truth,
or by fidelity in your duty." There was a political party in the State eschewing extremes, and
disliked equally by Whig and Tory, which went
by the name of the Trimmers. He refuses to
condemn them when he remembered Who it was

that blessed the peacemakers. "Acquaint yourselves" he writes again, though not bearing
altogether on politics, "with healing truths, and
labour to be as skilful in the work of pacifying
as most are in the work of dividing and disagreeing.
Know it to be a part of your Catholic work to be
peacemakers and therefore study to do it as a
workman that needeth not to be ashamed. Be
sure that you see the true state of the controversy,
and distinguish all that is merely verbal from
that which is material, and that which is about
methods and modes and circumstances from that
which is about substantial truths."

It is painful to think that this admirable man,
who was once thought good enough for a bishopric, which he declined, suffered imprisonment and
fines for conscience sake. As we have seen, he
could be severe enough and prejudiced enough in
his judgments, but as old age drew on he began to
acquaint himself "with healing truths," and to
banish controversy. He becomes a lover of good
men ; he pleads for a more general recognition of
the Holy Spirit, guiding life, purifying the heart
and instructing the conscience ; where the life of
the Spirit is manifest and the essential truths of the
Gospel are held, though a Church, and a Church
exercising discipline be necessary, it is vain to dispute about its form. With Episcopacy he has no
quarrel, and even Papists who trust Christ and
walk in such light as they have, shall be saved,
though he is sensible of the corruptions of their
Church and the groundless claims of the Pope. He
is ready to worship with Greeks, Lutherans, or

BAXTER AND BUNYAN

Ana-Baptists, if they will receive him, and he regards the divisions of Christians as the great outstanding scandal, and blames the bishops for not putting an end to it by the application of reasonable and Scriptural methods. He therefore favours the now common belief that there may be many folds (Churches particular), but only one flock (the Church Universal). His heart is pained with the condition of the heathen and Mohammedan world and the indifference of the Christian Churches to it, though he thinks there is more hope for the heathen than for the ungodly in a Christian land. He is content with the general sense of Scripture, as revealing man's sinfulness, God's love, and the way of Salvation ; so we may assume that modern questions of criticism would not have disturbed him, had they arisen. He laments all the harsh things he had spoken in controversy and asks God's and man's forgiveness for them. He suspects all history unless such as is written by impartial godly men, and these are rare, for even the godly zealot is more concerned to defend his side than to exhibit truth. He writes : " and withal I knew not how impatient divines were of being contradicted, nor how it would stir up all their powers to defend what they have once said, and to rise up against the truth which is thus thrust upon them, as the mortal enemy of their honour ! "[1] He is for dealing tenderly with honest doubt, since his own mind is not wholly free from aspects of it, and he favours the appeal to natural religion as a foundation. In early days his mind was occupied with his many

[1] "Self Review," p. 6.

sins and the state of his evil heart, which he constantly lamented; but now he thinks less about himself and more about God, a practice which he commends to others as productive of inward purity and sweet comfort.

It is not without a purpose so much of this estimable man is here revealed; for if, as Professor Bigg maintains, Baxter is the typical Puritan, his character, in most of its leading features, is that of the sane, broad-minded Christian Englishman of our day. The type is not extinct. The good seed has brought forth fruit a thousandfold. Those wishing for a fuller knowledge of Baxter cannot do better than procure a copy of his " Self-Review," edited with excellent notes and comments by Dr. Jayne, lately Bishop of Chester, a delightful work from which much in this chapter has been drawn.

CHAPTER XV

BAXTER cannot be considered, in any proper sense of the word, a politician ; yet both he and Bunyan may justly share with others the responsibility or the honour of diverting the stream of English politics from their old courses into the new channels in which they now flow. It is an arguable proposition whether Christian ministers should not abjure questions of State altogether, but no man in his senses would contend that they must be silent on the moral principles which ought to guide political life, or that the pastoral office involves the abnegation of citizenship. There was a time when the cleric ruled England, often with advantage, and he might do much, but in altered fashion, to rule it still, not from the hustings but from the pulpit, by the inculcation of the Christian virtues of moderation, justice, unselfishness, and brotherhood. Where these prevail the land is in peace. We have seen how the preaching of Wyclif's poor priests occasioned the Peasants' revolt ; not less certainly has the enfranchisement of the proletariat, with all its consequences, come as a natural result from such pulpits as that of Kidderminster and from the pages of the Pilgrim's Progress.

When the prophet has instilled into the minds of his hearers that men are involved in a common ruin and are the subjects of a common redemption, he has established a principle of equality which sooner or later must act as a solvent on class distinctions, or at least on class privileges, and from this it is but a step to the claim of common rights. Though Baxter and Bunyan had never breathed the word democracy it was latent in their message. Baxter deplores " the unhappiness of the nobility, gentry and great ones of the world, who live in such a temptation to sensuality, curiosity, and wasting of their time about a multitude of little things. . . . their pride, fulness of bread, and abundance of idleness and want of compassion for the poor ; and I more," he adds, " value the life of the poor labouring man ; but especially of him who hath neither poverty nor riches." Bunyan gives a matchless picture of the gay and selfish world, its heartlessness and thoughtlessness, in " Vanity Fair." Worldliness, self-interest, pride, avarice— all the sins of his day—appear in his marvellous gallery of portraits, and the contrast between them and the tender grace of the characters, from humble walks of life, who renounce earthly pomps and vanities and set their faces towards the celestial city, is most marked. Teaching of this kind must have sunk deep into the hearts of all who made acquaintance with it, and in time produced results which the teachers themselves may have little dreamed of ; as " many a shaft at random sent, finds mark the archer little meant."

Jeffreys, though the most unprincipled judge

England ever knew ; coarse, brutal and vindictive, was not deficient in ability and legal knowledge. Having toyed with Puritanism in its prosperity, he was well acquainted with its political tendencies. Baxter's trial is painful reading, but the shrewdness and perspicacity of the judge can be discovered in the violent outbursts with which he greeted counsel's defence of the accused. A passage having been read from one of Baxter's works stating " that great respect is due to those truly called bishops amongst us." " Aye," roared Jeffreys, " this is your Presbyterian cant, *truly* called to be bishops, that is of himself, and such rascals, called the bishops of Kidderminster, and other such places." " Baxter for bishops is a merry conceit indeed." He grossly misrepresented the case, it is true, but Jeffreys was quite right in maintaining that Baxter's conception of the Episcopate was far removed from that of the Court party and the dominant party in the Church ; and the political issue involved, as matters then stood, was radical, fundamental. Prelacy was the buttress of the absolutism of the crown. James, for all his buffoonery, was shrewd enough to see that as he understood kingship, " no bishop " meant " no King." " Sir," said Bishop Neile, " you are the breath of our nostrils." That was the type of bishop the Stuarts favoured, and though they were not all of the same mind—Usher, for instance, being a Puritan, the friend of Baxter, and probably the most learned divine in Europe—there was a sufficient number to uphold the preposterous claims, flattering alike to King and prelate, which

were based on the theory of the divine right of
Monarchs and the divine right of bishops. James
would not in his heart have admitted that those
two rights stood upon an equal footing, he was too
well versed in Presbyterian lore for that, but
he regarded prelacy as one might look upon the
outworks of a fortified city ; its fall might leave
his own position less secure.

Such was again the position of things when, in
1685, sixty years after the death of James the first,
Baxter stood before Jeffreys charged with sedition.
Here it may be remarked that to regard the opposition to prelacy either in England or in Scotland,
as merely a theological or historical question is
entirely to misapprehend the controversy. From
first to last it was far more a political question.
Monarchy and prelacy, as the subsequent course
of history has proved, were capable of resting on a
constitutional basis, and in that form they have
proved the most acceptable methods of government,
in Church and State, to the English people ; com-
patible with the widest religious and political
liberty. Under the Stuarts they were the instruments of tyranny. The nation was taxed against
its will and men were fined and imprisoned for
worshipping according to their conscience ; and
the English Episcopate was equally responsible
with the crown, in some instances more responsible,
for this state of things. After the Restoration
" the divine right " was a lost cause. Jeffreys may
rave as he will, but he cannot set it on its legs again.
The moderate or limited Episcopacy favoured by
Baxter and Usher, which if accepted might have

made English Christians one, and the constitutional Monarchy, which Baxter all along preferred to any other form of government—upholding it vehemently in Oliver's camp in his preachings to the soldiers, and in his discussions with the General— could not possibly be reconciled with the prerogatives which the Stuarts laid claim to, or with the conception of Episcopacy which possessed the minds of the Caroline bishops.

In his work "the Holy Commonwealth, a plea for the cause of Monarchy," which he no doubt meant as an irenicon, he, far from accomplishing his purpose, aroused the anger of Cavalier and Prelate to a white heat.   With all his heart Baxter was for a King, on this point his sincerity may not be questioned, but his King must be one who acknowledges that the laws of England are above the crown ; that Parliament is the highest court, where the personal will and word of the Monarch are not sufficient authority.   "Far better," writes Sir James Stephen, "to have roused against himself all the quills which had ever bristled on all the 'fretful porcupines' of theological strife " ; for the opinions which he here gives expression to are precisely those which were about to be proscribed with the return of the legitimate sovereign. But the student of those times, will not fail to note that it is the Monarchy of Baxter the Puritan, and not that of the furious Jeffreys, that England has found agreeable to its mind.   So long as the Stuart Kings and bishops held together and succeeded in imposing their will upon the nation, so long would liberty be withheld from the people and any form of

democratic rule be impossible. Under Baxter's
ideal monarchy the King was responsible to Parliament. Under James and Charles the King was
responsible to nobody. If we therefore dismiss
from our minds the bullying and hectoring of the
defendant by the judge and think only of the two
points of view, we shall see in the trial of Baxter
almost the last struggle between the old and the
new, and although Baxter retired from the contest
brow-beaten, consigned to a prison, and apparently
defeated, he was in reality the victor. Modern
England, under its constitutional and popular King,
enjoys such liberty as no other country can boast
of ; and the divine right of bishops has become a
purely academic question in which the general
public is not interested. In this matter we must
face facts ; and the facts, as we have hinted, are
that the position of the English Church as an Epis-
copally ordered institution, is due to political rather
than to theological considerations. At the same
time, whatever there may be in Episcopacy, a subject on which students will probably continue to
differ to the end of time, is as truly the possession
of the Anglican Communion as of any other Church
similarly organised. On this subject nothing wiser
has ever been said than those words of the learned
John Selden :—" There is no government enjoined
by example, but by precept ; it does not follow we
must have Bishops still, because we have had them
so long. They are equally mad who say Bishops
are so *Jure Divino* that they must be continued,
and they who say they are so Anti-Christian that
they must be put away. All is as the State pleases."

L

All is as the State pleases. That is " the case "
for Erastianism ; but to its Erastianism the English Church owes its freedom, its comprehensiveness
and its reasonableness.

Bunyan is largely " other world." Though
intensely human in his thought and in his characters, this world is not his home. He lived and
wrote at that period of the Puritan movement
when serious minds looked to heaven, not earth,
as their home ; when the evil world was a thing
to be endured not loved ; and, notwithstanding
his limitations, the honest Puritan of that day
was a far more admirable character, and certainly
a far better example to men whose minds are set
on righteousness, than the trading Sectary whom
we meet with after the Restoration.   This circumstance would be sufficient to account for the absence
of questions of politics from Bunyan's pages ; for
what concern had a man of his temper and outlook
with the affairs of the city of destruction ?   His
highest wisdom was to flee from it as Lot fled from
Sodom.

But if Bunyan was no political pamphleteer,
he has done his share in determining the political
outlook of the generations which came after him.
The burnings of Mary, the Wars of Alva, the
Inquisition, St. Bartholomew, have all helped the
cause of freedom in England ; the very last thing
their authors contemplated.   In like manner, the
persecutions of Stoughton's " Spiritual Heroes,"
and the long imprisonment of Bunyan, have profoundly affected English thought. So far as we
can regard anything in political life as permanent,

Englishmen have made up their minds that such things shall not happen again. The government of the country must be shaped so as to render them impossible. Thus far, the very pains and inconveniences suffered by men like Bunyan have turned out to our advantage as citizens. But, as has already been mentioned, almost every line that Bunyan wrote prepared the way for the " humanity-mongers," and for a truer conception of the common relationships which ought to exist between man and man ; in a word, for the demo-cratic age which was already rapidly undermining the feudal.

Bunyan as a theologian and a writer of English does not greatly concern us here, but to anyone interested in him from such points of view, Pro-fessor Dowden's sketch, in " Puritan and Anglican" will be found eminently just and sympathetic. The popular view of Bunyan, formed mainly on Macaulay's essay, is there judiciously and cour-teously corrected ; his religious views and feelings are explained, as well as Macaulay's inability to deal with them ; and his natural ability and mastery of forceful Saxon English fully appre-ciated.

As an influence on religious thought he is far removed from Baxter, the difference helping to illustrate the highly variegated character of Puri-tanism, but it is much wider and will probably last longer. Baxter might have been a bishop of the English Church, and his learning would have adorned a deanery. To think of Bunyan in either capacity provokes a smile ; yet, while the " Saint's

Rest," the "Self Review," and two popular
hymns, remain as the only lasting monuments of
Baxter's piety—all his great works rest on the
shelves of the curious, gathering dust—" The Holy
War," " Grace Abounding," and " The Pilgrim's
Progress," are assured of life so long as a British
Empire and an English speaking people remain on
the earth.   As for the " Pilgrim's Progress," it is
become, perhaps next to the Bible, every man's
book.   Long ago the nations of Europe have made
their translations of it, and few years pass without
witnessing its entrance, through the enterprise of
one or other of our missionary societies, into some
Eastern country or among some African tribe,
while the English public continue to welcome it,
in some new dress, handsomely bound and copiously
illustrated, with the coming of each Christmas
season.

Nor must we forget that while what remains to
us, or is available for general use, of Baxter, is
mostly for the cultured few, Bunyan is for the
many.   The little " Bethels " and " Ebenezers "
in the back streets of our towns and in remote
villages and hamlets all over England, bearing a
close resemblance to the original modest chapel in
Bedford, remind us that Bunyan was a preacher
of the Word as well as a writer.   These humble
houses of prayer, as well as our great national
Church, have their part to play in sanctifying the
life and the homes of England ; one day we may
see Cathedral and Bethel united in a more glorious
English Church than either Stuart bishop or
Puritan preacher dreamed of ; until that day come,

and as a means to its coming, each party would do well to cultivate a just appreciation of the other's work. But, whether it come or stay, the wayside meeting house and the immortal Pilgrim are ever present to sweeten thought and promote righteousness, and to proclaim that Bunyan, though dead yet speaketh.

CHAPTER XVI

THE PURITAN AS EDUCATIONIST : REMARKS ON THE QUAKERS

INASMUCH as education is closely allied to religion, and must affect profoundly both political and social life, it has long been a matter of regret to many Englishmen that their country is not yet in possession of a complete national system of education, covering every department of human knowledge ; and that what we have is very costly and far from perfect. It would require a very nice discrimination to apportion the blame for this state of things amongst those who appear to be responsible. But we may hazard the opinion that if there had not been a small fanatical section in the ranks of Puritan nonconformity, repudiating Cromwell's aphorism that " the care of religion is the duty of the State," and a very large reactionary section in the Established Church, we might by this time have covered the land with elementary schools of a uniform type, in which every child might be taught essential Christianity, in addition to receiving secular instruction suitable to its capacity. But, the State lacking courage and the churches charity, the child goes forth to the world with the better part of its nature imperfectly developed. If we gave attention to the fact that

the youth of England in each generation must soon
be leaders in the churches, if not lost to them by
our quarrels, and the electors of our Parliaments,
and consequently determining, to that extent, the
character of our religion and our politics, we
might be inclined to improve our educational
methods. The ideal educationalist, aiming at
making good citizens rather than good denomina-
tionalists, is perfectly in line with Cromwell, Milton,
and the Society of Friends; he has entered into
their labours. Milton, in his " Small Tractate of
Education to Mr. Hartlib," confines himself to the
education of gentlefolk. Great soul though he was,
and friend of the people, he was something of an
aristocrat. His curriculum takes away our breath ;
yet there is not one word in it suggestive of party
preference. His strictures on our Universities
anticipate Mills' trenchant condemnation : " Ignorant the youths come to them," says Mills ;
" and ignorant they go away."[1] He will have no
specialising; between the ages of twelve and
twenty-one the whole ground must be covered—
Classics, Hebrew, Science, Logic, Music, Botany,
Anatomy, Elementary Medicine, Fencing, Wrest-
ling, Fortification, Architecture, Law, Politics,
Engineering, Navigation, Modern Languages, and,
above all, Religion, find each a place ; and every
youth must learn soldiering, that he may be ready,
if need requires, to defend his country. We do
not possess Mr. Hartlib's reply, if there is one,
but we hope he was satisfied. " I call therefore,"

---

[1] Inaugural address by J. S. Mill.

writes Milton, " a compleat and generous education
that which fits a man to perform justly, skilfully
and magnanimously, all the offices both private
and publick, of Peace and War."

Milton's idea of the end of learning was as lofty
as the course he prescribes was broad, manly, and
noble. " The end then to learning," he proceeds,
" is to repair the ruin of our first parents, by re-
gaining to know God aright, and out of that knowledge to love Him, to imitate Him, to be like Him,
as we may the nearest by possessing our souls of
true virtue, which being united to the heavenly
grace of faith, makes up the highest perfection."
But while filled with admiration of his scheme and
his hopes, it must be admitted that like many
Puritans of his day he miscalculated human nature.
We can imagine the average healthy boy of twelve,
as he peruses the exhaustive programme provided
for his benefit, exclaiming with Job, " Let the day
perish wherein I was born." The " academies "
with their hundred and fifty pupils in each, never
came to birth, but the grand conception may remind us that the Puritan aimed at making us a
godly, learned, and politically wise people ; and
also that, but for the unreasonableness of English
Christians, the aim might have been in large
measure attained.   Cromwell, not less than Milton,
was an ardent supporter of learning.   Frederick
Harrison, who has an enthusiastic but judicious
admiration for Cromwell, in a summary of the
great acts of the Protector, after informing us
that " he made some of the best judges England
ever had.   Justice and law opened a new era,"

goes on to relate how greatly his rule favoured
learning. " Education was reorganised ; the
Universities reformed ; Durham founded. It is
an opponent who says, ' All England over these
were halcyon days.' Men of learning of all opinions
were encouraged and befriended. ' If there was
a man in England who excelled in any faculty or
science, the Protector would find him out, and
reward him according to his merit.' It was the
Protector's brother-in-law, Warden of Wadham
College, who there gathered together the group
which ultimately founded the Royal Society."[1]
Concurrently with the spread of education was
the encouragement of Missions to the Heathen
and to the Colonists. The fact is often overlooked
that the original " Society for the Propagation
of the Gospel in Foreign Parts " was a Puritan
foundation, greatly favoured by Oliver and the
Independents.

The Quakers, as already stated, may properly
be numbered amongst the Puritan Sectaries,
although persecuted, both in England and America,
by other Puritans who might have learned mercy
by the things they themselves had suffered for
conscience sake. And here may be noted, though
it be a digression, their address to James the Second
at his accession, truly a masterpiece of *naïveté*.
James, though a Roman Catholic, was ostensibly
a member of the Church of England, honestly
believed to be such by the common people, though
it would be hard to say the same of the bishops.

---

[1] F. Harrison, " Oliver Cromwell," p. 216.

The Quakers were under no delusion on the subject, and from their erratic founder, " the man in the leather breeches," had learned the habit of great plainness of speech. " We are come," they say, " to testify our sorrow for the death of our good Friend Charles, and our joy for thy being made our Governor. We are told thou art not of the persuasion of the Church of England no more than we ; therefore we hope that thou wilt grant us the same liberty which thou allowest thyself."[1] Their good friend Charles had, on more than one occasion, shown them more kindness than they had met at the hands of the fanatics amongst the Sectaries ; and they quite naturally hoped for an extension of kingly favour under the rule of his brother. Charles, a good-humoured voluptuary, may have found them and their eccentricities more interesting than the long sermons he had endured in Scotland, and the Court flatteries of Whitehall, which he indolently accepted but had too much sense to believe in ; but it is impossible that James could ever have understood them, yet for political reasons of his own he found it convenient to grant to them and others, for a time, a measure of tolerance which they were wise enough to accept and make good use of, while it lasted. It is true the Church clergy and the majority of the Non- conformists, fearing James even when bearing gifts, did not avail themselves of a liberty which was designed to bring in Popery, but the Quakers and, according to Stoughton,[2] many Independent

---

[1] De Rapin, " History of England," XV. p. 8.
[2] Stoughton, " Spiritual Heroes," p. 367.

congregations, accepted it thankfully rather as the gift of heaven than of the king.

Every occasion which made their situation easier was employed by this singular people in promoting in their own way the good of the people. From the first they lamented the prevailing ignorance of the rural dwellers, and resolved, though they were the smallest Nonconformist community in the country, to enlighten them.

It would take much time to set forth the part Quakers have taken, in their peculiarly unostentatious way, in furthering education amongst the poor. Although they steadfastly maintain that human learning, by which of course they mean scholarship, is " not essential to a Gospel minister,"[1] they admit that it can be made highly useful should the minister possess it ; and from their earliest days they have been distinguished for making " provision for the support and education of the poor." Penn's colony in America had not a single illiterate person amongst the white population, and though no Quaker aspired to a scheme of education equal to Milton's, the whole Society placed the cultivation of the intellect next to the knowledge of God. This is no less than what might be looked for in a community holding the awful truth that the inner light of the Eternal Spirit shines in every human soul ; the temple therefore must be freed of darkness that it may be a fit receptacle of so mighty a Guest. We have seen of what a rude egotism some of those early Quakers were, and it is much to the credit of their

---

[1] Tuke, " Quaker Principles," p. 97.

successors that this unpleasant feature is not
denied ;[1] yet, though the outer aspect is now
changed, no change has taken place in the spiritual
principles which gave originality and life to the
movement from the beginning. They still maintain that the truly valid ministry is one directly
called of God, a ministry unremunerated and not
separated from the congregation or from a secular
calling ; that the sacraments are spiritual, not
material, a silent, unseen work in the inner man;
that worship is under the influence and direct
guidance of the Holy Spirit, and therefore a silent
meeting is not less profitable than a vocal ; that
war is un-Christian. To these it may be added
that their interest in the education of the nation,
though circumstances are changed, remains as
strong as ever. The British schools (undenominational) were largely maintained by the Society.
Forster who, as Minister of Education, gave the
country Board Schools in 1871, came of a Quaker
stock, and was educated at a well-known Quaker
school at Tottenham. Groups of Quakers raised
funds for the education of the blind, and sent
teachers amongst them into several English counties ; while a most interesting and valuable work
originated with some members of the Society
about thirty years ago, and flourishes still under
the name of " Sunday Morning Schools," in which
working men whose education had been neglected
in their youth, are taught reading, writing, and
arithmetic ; the mundane lesson being always
followed by reading of Scripture, discussion, and

---

[1] Hodgkin, " Quaker Saints."

prayer. The genuine Quaker, wherever you meet him, is invariably the enemy of ignorance ; and, small as the Society of Friends is, and from the nature of its tenets must remain, its line is gone out through all the earth and its words to the end of the world. Its influence as a religious force is still considerable, for it has a message all its own for the sons of men, which the Society alone is capable of imparting. Many can walk in Saul's armour, but few can handle David's sling. Up to quite recent times the Friends followed the Whigs in politics ; Liberalism might always count on the Quaker vote, and if ever those gentle, self-controlled people lost their tempers and permitted themselves the luxury of a red-hot outburst (and it must be admitted such occasions were rare) it was during the stormy period of a General Election. In recent times, however, they have made the discovery that all the virtues, or vices, as the case may be, are not on one side, and their considerable political influence is exercised mainly in promoting, with either party indifferently, the kingdom of God and the good of mankind.

This fact is practically an admission that ' Friends,' as they prefer to call themselves, are not in our days orthodox, politically ; they are as averse from a political creed as from a religious ; and herein it may be said lies their great value to the nation's politics. They set an example that may well be copied of following the good in every party, while refusing to be brought under bondage to any. Whether this attitude of detachment from political parties can be followed

in the matter of religion is doubtful, yet Friends
who in their early days, as Mr. Tuke points out,
accepted nearly all the views of the Sectaries
except Calvinism, in more recent times have
claimed a freedom which would have alarmed
their ancestors. It is true that Penn, in his book
" The Sandy Foundation Shaken," gave expression
to most unorthodox opinions, but his was ever a
wayward mind, and up to quite recent times the
generally accepted Evangelical doctrines were
held and taught by the majority of Friends
in England. In America, however, a schism of
a serious and extensive character has taken
place, and has not yet yielded to the healing
remedies which have been applied to it. Nevertheless both in the Republic and at home, the
presence of ' Friends ' is regarded on every hand
as an influence entirely wholesome and sound.
Lovers of good works and of good men ; patrons
of learning ; advocates of temperance, of toleration, of law and order, of unity among Christians ;
promoters of Missions to the heathen ; ardent
social workers, it would be difficult now to think
of a time when they were not, and most certainly
their disappearance from our social order, if we
can imagine it, would leave a blank impossible
to fill up. They have often been first in hitting
a blot in our social life and in giving a wise lead
to reformers. The Bible Society, which provides
a platform of unity altogether unique, owes them
much since the day a Gurney of Earlham persuaded a bishop of Norwich to preside at its
Annual Meeting. Since that day we have travelled

far and seldom indeed has the Quaker, whenever he has been our leader, pointed in a wrong direction.

We shall meet these people again before our work is done. For the present it is sufficient to say that education being something more than attendance at School and learning to read and write—conversation, association in work, social service, and a hundred other things which contribute to the formation of character, may properly be regarded as education—Puritans, and not least among them the Society of Friends, continue, as of old, their education of the nation, and thus to influence the course of our political and religious life. Wherever the Puritan influence weakens there the people fail, religion is often abandoned altogether or becomes formal and outward, and political idealism is overborne by motives of self interest, frequently leading to acts of violence.

CHAPTER XVII

LATER ASPECTS OF PURITANISM

SIR JAMES STEPHEN gives a dismal picture of the
religious condition of England in the early days
of Puritanism, a condition which he attributes
to the Church's neglect of its duty. The Tudor
and Caroline divines may have been very well in
their way—for however distasteful the politics
and the theology of the latter may have been to
the majority of the English people, many of them
upheld the tradition *clerus Anglicanus stupor
mundi*—yet at the best they spoke to a
limited audience. The masses were beyond their
reach and little was done for them. The peasant
could understand Latimer, but Bishop Andrewes
with his quips and puns and Latin tags would
have been incomprehensible. Even Baxter did
not disclaim these methods in his controversial
writings, nor can we agree with the opinion that
" literature is wholly free from this folly " even
in our day. Lockhart, for instance, gave as his
reason for resigning the Editorship of the Quarterly
Review that he was

> " Over-worked and over-worried,
> Over-Crockered and over-Murrayed."

---

[1] Essay on Baxter.

But all this is by the way. It must, however, in a general way, be admitted that so far as the English Church was concerned " to the poor the Gospel was not preached " in those days, and Stephen's contention that the Puritan alone kept the flame of piety alight amongst the poor holds good to some extent. But in his depreciation of the Church of England, he somewhat overlooks the fact that many of the clergy were as deeply imbued with the Puritan spirit and Puritan divinity as were any of the ministers of the Sectaries, and proclaimed ' the doctrines of grace ' as vehemently and as persuasively as the preachers in Cromwell's Camp. Nor should we forget that those Anglican Puritans were the forerunners of the great spiritual Revival of the 18th century, a movement which touched the common life of England as nothing before it or since has touched it, and, in Wesley's words, spread Scriptural holiness throughout the land. In the opinion of two at least of our historians, Wesley saved the country from the horrors of a revolution similar to that of France. From Anglican Puritanism also has come that Evangelical piety which has spread to the remotest parts of the Empire. At the same time an impartial mind may easily agree with Stephen when, in words as true as they are wise and generous, he tells us that " Whatever may have been the faults, or whatever the motives, of the Protector, there can be no doubt that under his sway England witnessed a diffusion, till then unknown, of the purest influence of genuine religious principles. The popular historians of

M

that period, from various motives, have dis-
guised or misrepresented the fact; and they who
derive their views on this subject from Clarendon,
from Hume, or from Hudibras, mistake a caricature for a genuine portrait."[1]   The fact is the
English peasantry would have been in heathen
darkness but for Puritanism.

As the years passed, new forces came into play
and new thoughts took possession of the minds of
students and men of leisure.   Bacon, Hobbes, the
Royal Society, Newton and the Latitudinarians
brought a new spirit into the kingdom and into
the world.   So far as this spirit affected religion,
and it affected it much, as may be seen in the tolerant
and mildly sceptical views of men so different
as Chillingworth and Jeremy Taylor, it tended
toward a common faith or a common Church,
which should embrace good and just men of every
ecclesiastical colour, a Church "as wide as human
life and as deep as human need."   And who shall
say that such a Church would have been un-
acceptable to Cromwell and the wiser spirits
amongst his Independent Friends ?   Rationalism
in this equitable and temperate form did not,
any more than the Restoration, destroy Puritanism.   It simply set it in its proper place.   Cromwell, it is true, towards the close of his life seeing
clearly enough the direction in which the current
of thought was setting, and failing a settlement,
religious and political, which he earnestly desired,
but which the discordant elements in the Army
and the Parliament made impossible, was obliged

[1] Essay on Baxter, p. 86.

to fall back on the phrases of his earlier days,
and the saints are once more 'a peculiar people,'
'a remnant,' a fragment among the nation at
large. Nevertheless all that was of worth in the
great movement survived its leaders and its
enemies, and even the scientific studies and
discoveries which for the moment seemed to act
as a solvent on its theology. As regards such
discoveries it is of interest to note in passing that
men of science in the last two centuries, who have
been definitely religious, have found their spiritual
home chiefly amongst Puritans ; Faraday joined
the Glassites, a very Evangelical sect; Lord Kelvin
was a devout Evangelical; Romanes, won by a
zealous ritualist from agnosticism to a somewhat
limited but sincere profession of Christianity,
rested in the simplest forms of devotion ; while
at the University it is often an eminent scientist
who is found presiding at the meetings of the
Bible Society, the Temperance Society, or some
other cause of a decidedly Puritan origin.

Returning to the Restoration period we find
that after that event, the farmers and traders
who formed the army of the New Model went
back to their old occupations and were known
by no other sign than their greater sobriety and
industry. A very clear proof that they did not
despair of their principles. " When Puritanism
laid down the sword," writes Green,[1] " and ceased
from the attempt to build up a kingdom of God
by force and violence, it fell back on its truer
work of building up a kingdom of Righteousness

---

[1] History of English People, Vol. III.

in the hearts and consciences of men. It was
from the moment of its seeming fall that its real
victory began. As soon as the wild orgy of the
Restoration was over men began to see that
nothing that was really worthy in the work of
Puritanism had been undone."

An almost similar statement might be made
with regard to Politics. The ideal of the more
advanced Puritan politicians, such as Vane,
Bradshaw, Haslerig, and indeed all the great
Parliamentarians, was not established until the
time of Pitt; but it was openly professed and
preached by all of them, and, as we have seen, slept
in the great saying of Pym, that "the Commons
must save the nation alone." The fixed idea of
those men was "to establish the autocracy of an
elected House, supreme over the Executive, and
free from any constitutional limit, just as we see
it to-day."[1]

If these studies had no other purpose than to
establish the fact, for fact we believe it to be,
that modern England is both on its political and
religious side the creation of Puritanism, they
might end here; but the case for that mighty
movement would be incomplete if we failed to
trace its influence down to our times.

It was one of the rash statements of Macaulay
that the Church of England since the Reformation had furnished but one saint, the great,
single-hearted, scholar missionary, Henry Martyn.
Surely much depends on what is meant by a
saint, or whether good men, such as the English

---

[1] F. Harrison, "Cromwell," p. 186.

Church produces in plenty, are not better than saints. The late Father Tyrrell, a Jesuit, in an outburst that seems to come from a heart quite broken, speaks thus of the English Church, "Church of my fathers, Church of better than saints, why did I ever leave you?"[1] We may be content with the description. England would not exchange its Ridley, its Jewell, its Andrewes, its Hooker, its Taylor, its Herbert, and many another good man, for all the saints of the Romish Calendar. England would not barter the Tudor divines—that is if England or the modern English clergy knew them, which is not the case—with "their strong masculine sense and their incomparable learning"[2] for all the divinity of Abbé Migne's library. The type of minister England loves is one who will buy truth at any cost and sell it not; who will have nothing to do with mental reservations, who scorns intellectual dishonesty. It will pardon much in such a man and follow where he leads. Such a man the country found in John Wesley. May we claim Wesley as a Puritan? Canon Overton in a not too sympathetic, yet on the whole just appreciation of him, says we may not.[3] The truth is Wesley is too big a man for either neutral or partisan to paint. When he speaks of the Stuarts he is a Jacobite or non-juror, when he turns to Swift or Sterne he is a Puritan of Puritans. Poor Sterne, who was a kind-hearted creature

---

[1] Miss Petre, " Father Tyrrell Life."
[2] Archbishop Benson.
[3] Overton, " Evangelical Revival," pp. 44, 172.

for all his faults, is rent in pieces by this severe moralist.[1] Whatever Wesley was in himself, and we need not risk a judgment on the point, there can be no doubt that the movement he inaugurated and led for fifty years was a Puritan movement of a most pronounced character ; himself an autocrat he founded and ruled a spiritual democracy. So many lives of Wesley are available, together with his marvellous journal, that anything more than a brief survey is unnecessary here. Born and brought up in an English Vicarage, with a stern, just and Godly father, and a mother whose natural abilities and deep piety have rarely been surpassed, he enjoyed advantages granted to few youths. He went up to Oxford well versed, for one of his age, in the strictest views of English Church divinity and ceremonial. An excellent scholar, on graduating he was elected to a fellowship at Lincoln College, and began sometime later with a few like-minded men, to live a severely disciplined religious life, reading the Greek Testament together, observing a rule of fasting, receiving the Holy Communion weekly in Chapel, and visiting the poor and the prisoners in the city ; a course of life which exposed them to the ridicule of the thoughtless and gay young men, who formed the vast majority of the students in the Universities in those days. He undertook a mission to Georgia where he strove to impose his views and practices on an unwilling and rather worldly congregation, with such small success

---

[1] Wesley's Journal (abridged), p. 370.

that he felt obliged to relinquish his post and return to England. Through all this time Wesley, for all his devoutness and extreme conscientiousness, was what may fairly be described as a ' legalist.' Looking back on this period he doubted if at that time he was converted. We may dismiss the doubt, whilst fully recognising that to the joyful aspects of Christianity, to that freedom wherewith Christ makes His disciples free, he was undoubtedly a stranger up to the time of his intercourse with the Moravians, from whom he learned much that was helpful. In his intercourse with them he learned experimental religion, a personal knowledge of God, the Saviour and Friend of men, and an assurance of forgiveness. This latter was, in Wesley's day, a distinctively Calvinistic tenet, though Wesley himself was throughout life an Arminian. Wesley's message to the small traders and working classes, for to them chiefly he was sent, was simple. Repentance whereby sin is forsaken, full trust in Christ's Atonement to cancel trangression, the gift of the Spirit of Power to every believer. It was in fact the Reformers' and Hooker's ' justification by Faith ' which was in his Prayer Book and Articles all the time, but which he failed to realise in the days when he served God in the oldness of the letter. The acceptance of the Evangelical position, in which for him and his brother the two sacraments had a definite position as means of grace, changed him from a servant to a son, gave him a religion of joy and freedom instead of a religion of servitude. Confident

that he had something worth offering to his
country, blessed with a strong constitution, sound
learning, good judgment and great organising
powers and, we may add, never in the enjoyment
of "Isaac's pure blessing and a verdant home,"
he goes forth 'strong in the Lord' taking the
world as his parish. After fifty years of strenuous
labours in all parts of England, and in many
parts of Wales, Scotland and Ireland, Wesley
yields up his life exclaiming 'Best of all God is
with us' and singing with faltering voice "I'll
praise my Maker while I've breath."

It was his custom to rise at four o'clock each
morning, and often he had preached to anxious
crowds before sunrise. He read, prayed, composed sermons, and thought out plans of evangelisation as he rode on horse-back from town to
town. Through scorching heat, through storm
and tempest, through darkest nights, climbing
steep paths, fording swollen rivers; mocked,
cursed, stoned, led before justices, opposed by
his own Church, he ran his godly race. Perhaps
on the whole it was to the country's advantage
that the ecclesiastical powers, with the exception
of a few favourably disposed bishops and vicars,
opposed him. The opposition sent him into
'highways and hedges,' into the streets and lanes
of the cities. There he found his congregations
who drank in the life-giving Word and cried out
"What must we do to be saved?" The Reformation in England, great as it was in intellect
and learning—"to read those later Tudor theologians," said one, "is like feeding on the marrow

of lions "—great in the wisdom with which it combined the old and the new, was less of a spiritual movement than this Revival of the Eighteenth Century. We must get back to Apostolic days to find a parallel. Wesleyanism and the Evangelical Revival in the English Church found England a spiritual wilderness, and left it a watered garden.

Wesley no doubt was irregular in some of his methods ; he broke through conventional order ; he sometimes intruded into parishes where a ' faithful witness ' ministered and he was not needed. There are spots on the sun ; and the Apostle of toiling and middle class England cannot be pronounced absolutely blameless in all his doings. Yet it seems somewhat childish to criticise a man and a movement which wrought a moral change in England that has altered for the better both its social and political life, and probably saved it from anarchy and bloodshed. "Church or no church," said Wesley, "the people must be saved."

The characteristic note of early Methodism was its joyfulness. This was expressed chiefly in the hymns of Charles Wesley, which were caught up and sung by multitudes of men and women as fast as they appeared, and they appeared to the number of over six thousand. All the nation broke into song ; and the songs—a rare thing—contained " the whole counsel of God "—a whole body of sober, sound, Scriptural divinity. Before parting with Wesley, a word must be said about his relation to the Church of England. He never left it, and would gladly have seen his great Society safely housed within it; nevertheless from the day on which he felt his " heart strangely warmed," at the little meeting of believers in Aldersgate Street, in 1738, there was a complete break with his past. Baptism may be the means of incorporation into the visible Church, but the gift of the Spirit is to Faith. And what meaning can be attached to Apostolic succession by one who declares, " I firmly believe I am a scriptural ἐπίσκοπος as much as any man in England or in Europe ; for the uninterrupted succession I know to be a fable, which no man ever did or can prove ? " Indeed, the eulogist of Marcus Aurelius and of Ignatius Loyola, the censor of the " execrable wretches " who wrangled at the early Church councils, the man who refused to believe a brother who joined the Church of Rome had changed his religion, may fairly be claimed by Dean Stanley as the founder of the broad Church party, a claim, by the way, already made for Baxter in these pages.

But wherever we may set this prophet of God in the schools of theologians, one great fact of his life remains, the fact of a mighty religious organisation dispersed throughout the Anglo-Saxon world, Evangelical in its doctrine, democratic in its politics, loyal and submissive to the ruling powers of State, and full of mercy and good works.

" I read the newspaper," said Wesley, " that I may see how God is ruling the world." In Wesley's campaign and its development, rather than in the writings of historians, favourable or the reverse, the wise Englishman will read how God is ruling the Church universal.

CHAPTER XVIII

IT seems a self-evident proposition that politics
and religion, in England, at any rate, cannot be
separated. They touch at so many points that
the political barometer of a party rises or falls
with the progress or decline of the religious body
most in sympathy with it. A brief examination
of the great spiritual movement in the English
Church, known as the Evangelical Revival, is
therefore necessary to an understanding of many
important events in the political history of the
nineteenth century. The English Evangelicals
are, in doctrine, successors of the Reformation
fathers and the early Puritan clergy. They have
never been favoured with what journalists call a
good Press, and it is to their credit that they have
not cultivated the art of self-advertisement. The
Church papers did not greatly bless them ; some
journals have even adopted the worldly-wise
policy of damning them with faint praise. Large-
minded historians, like Lecky, have done them
justice, and a good statement of their work and
influence will be found in Stock's admirable history
of the Church Missionary Society ; but the popular
Church historian, who perhaps cannot help writing
with a bias, and is therefore of all historians least

reliable, after a few pages of commendation generally concludes with animadversions on what he considers their limitations. To those who have drawn their opinions from writers of this class, Balleine's "History of the Evangelical Party" and Ryle's "Christian Leaders" may be recommended as giving a more sympathetic view. Deficient in the temper, in the arts and graces, which commend men to the Episcopal mind, they are rarely popular with the higher authorities in the Church, though essentially loyal and law-abiding; and, in recent times, they have often displayed such a yielding and almost pusillanimous spirit, and such a lack of unity when their own principles have been challenged, that we need not be surprised at their being described as "the tattered remnant of a broken and defeated army;" or that a brilliant and broad-minded dignitary, when it was suggested to him that he should become their leader, replied, but not with malice, "Their leader! You cannot lead a rabble." Sympathetically judged, all this is in their favour. Men whose aims are directly spiritual will not easily be induced to combine for purely party purposes. As a matter of fact, the few party societies which are associated with the Evangelical School, have been from the first engaged solely in a war of defence, not of aggression; and though, in carrying it on, they have shown an extraordinary lack of worldly prudence and a most remarkable facility for putting themselves in the wrong, their purpose has been honest. Perhaps they get comfort in the thought that children of light are not proverbially wise in their generation.

While recognising the Puritan origin of both the Wesleyan and the Evangelical movements, we must not confound them, for though they had much in common and were to some extent inter-dependent, they differed fundamentally in some matters. Wesley honestly desired to keep his Society within the borders of the National Church, but many of his converts were nominal members of other communities before they came under his influence, communities which had, in common with the Church, lost their first love, and lapsed into formalism or Socinianism. Other circum-stances wrought with this to give a direction to the movement which Wesley never contemplated. Let writers, then, say what they may, it was inevitable from the first that Wesleyanism must, sooner or later, find a home of its own. Too much has been made, by Macaulay and others, of the Church's failure to retain them. The fault, if fault it was, was neither wholly that of the Church nor of Wesley himself. The separation of that vast community, whose present membership in its various ramifications outnumbers considerably that of the whole Anglican Communion, into an organisation of its own, was due almost entirely to the working of natural causes. For Wesleyanism to do its work and give its message to the world, freedom of movement was essential, and the National Church in the eighteenth century was incapable, and is to-day incapable, of giving the necessary freedom and of accommodating itself to the needs of such a society. It was not, then, altogether the Church's lack of sympathy or its persecuting spirit, but its very nature and constitution which hindered absorption. The new wine would have burst the old bottles ; and in spite of Macaulay's brilliant periods, the difficulty would have been ten-fold greater in the Church of Rome, Wesley and his followers being what they were.

Again, Wesley and his officers were uncompromising Arminians. Christ had tasted death for every man, and willed all men to be saved. One of their most popular hymns contained the lines :

" For all my Lord was crucified,
For all, for all, my Saviour died."

Life or death was in the choice of every soul to whom the Gospel was preached.

And as regards politics. though Wesley and his brothers meddled little in such matters, the sympathies of the Society were early manifested in behalf of the Whigs, and in more recent times in behalf of the radical party.

Here, then, were points of difference enough with the Evangelicals in the Church. The Evangelical clergy were staunch Churchmen, claiming, and with good reason, to be of all parties the truest representatives of its doctrine and ceremonial. The Church was Apostolic and Catholic, but it was also Reformed and Protestant. The highest Churchmen in the seventeenth and eighteenth centuries had no quarrel with any of these terms. On no consideration would the Evangelical party quit the Church of their fathers.

If Wesley founded the society of people called Methodists, George Whitfield may be regarded as the first leader of the Evangelical party in the English Church ; and Whitfield abhorred Arminianism. All the early Evangelicals were moderate Calvinists. They held the doctrine of election, but not of reprobation. This is not the place to discuss such questions, but it may be remarked that they are as akin to philosophy as to theology. Calvinism and Arminianism are determinism and free-will under other names ; and are as old as human thought. It has been pointed out humorously, by more than one critic of the National Church, that nothing is more indicative of its growing intellectual poverty than the matters about which Churchmen quarrel. A hundred and fifty years ago deep questions of philosophy engaged their minds, and were ably dealt with on both sides ; to-day congregations are entertained with disputes about copes and chasubles, holy water and wafers. The criticism is severe and somewhat unfair ; the pity is that there is some truth in it. A caustic saying of H. L. Massingham's is worth quoting in this connection : " If anyone should ask why this age has forgotten Christ, the answer should be because it changes the wine of life into peppermint water."

Again, the Evangelical Church party took the Conservative or Tory side in politics. Here and there a Whig might be found in it, but he was regarded as something of a curiosity. The only section which definitely ranged itself on the Whig side was the broad Church party. The High

Churchmen, the Evangelicals and the Low Churchmen were all, with rare exceptions, on the Tory
side. To minds detached from parties or having
little interest in them, minds more interested in
measures than in men, the advantages of dividing
the greatest moral force of the age between the
two political parties in the country will be at once
recognised; the Methodists amongst the Whigs
and the Evangelicals amongst the Tories. A
conscious righteousness, a spiritual force, was
added to each party, and the resulting benefit
to the country has been very great. We shall
see, on occasions when great moral issues are involved, both parties laying aside their hostilities,
for the time, and combining for the attainment
of justice. There is nothing more honourable in
English politics than action of this kind; and that
it is frequently taken is due in large measure to
the circumstance that both parties have received
into their ranks a considerable element of Evangelical Puritanism.

Wesley and Whitfield differed so much on the
question of Calvinism that for a long time they
stood apart. Hard things were said on both sides,
Wesley going so far as to state in one of his sermons
that Calvinism made God worse than the devil;
so easy is it in heats of controversy to misrepre-
sent what we dislike. As a matter of fact, the
mild Calvinism of the English divines and of the
Evangelicals was found to be a doctrine very full
of comfort to those who accepted it; and it did
not, as Wesley seemed to fear, abate in the smallest
degree their Evangelistic zeal. Whitfield himself,

though a strong predestinationist, was entirely uninfluenced by it in the way Wesley held to be inevitable. No man ever earned a better title to the blessing promised to those " who sow beside all waters." As many as twenty thousand miners are said to have come out to listen to his field sermons, and as he discoursed on the doctrine of the Cross, setting forth salvation through faith in the merits of Christ, the tears made little white gutters in their grimy faces, and hundreds turned to God in penitence and continued steadfast to their lives' end.

Selina, Countess of Huntingdon, provided Whit- field with a very different kind of congregation from the miners of Kingswood. In her drawing- room might be seen the Prince of Wales and the Duke of Cumberland, Lord North and the Earl of Chatham, Walpole, Chesterfield, the Duchess of Marlborough and others of their rank and class, who came to hear the Gospel from Whitfield and other preachers whom their hostess procured for their benefit.[1] In many cases the impressions produced were deep and lasting. The Earl of Dartmouth, one of the most learned and cultured men of the day, threw in his lot unconditionally with the party. The cold-hearted Chesterfield was deeply moved. Fashionable ladies became con- cerned about deeper things than balls and routs and theatres. The sceptical Benjamin Franklin confessed that, after one of Whitfield's sermons, he was so overcome that he emptied the contents of his pocket into the collecting plate.

---

[1] Balleine's " History of the Evangelical Party," p. 57.

In London, where the Evangelicals held but three livings, a great work was carried on. Lecture-ships, to which preachers were appointed by the laity, and proprietary chapels built by private individuals, gave the serious clergy their opportunity. Scholars like Romaine, cultured preachers like Venn and Richard Cecil, drew large congregations wherever they preached. The Lock Hospital Chapel and some dozen other places of worship were crowded with worshippers every Sunday, many people having to stand throughout the whole service in one or other of these places. A new life began to stir in the Mother Church of the land ; and the great mass of the people, which throughout the Restoration period and the dead years that followed had remained Puritan at heart, welcomed with joy and tears the old Evangel which told of pardon, peace and power. This new Puritanism, as we may call it, was very unlike the Puritanism of Cromwell's day. The Gospel was the same, but it came in a new dress and from a new type of preacher. The marvellous fire and eloquence of Whitfield mingled in him with a tenderness of feeling which bowed and broke the hearts even of hearers who came to criticise. Gentleness, reasonableness, persuasiveness and a great yearning for souls marked the movement from its rise. The results baffle description. Scarcely a sermon was preached without signs following ; often a whole congregation was brought under deep conviction of sin. The prayer in Cowper's hymn received abundant answer :

> " O rend the heavens, come quickly down,
> And make a thousand hearts Thine own."

It is difficult to realise the rapid spread of this great awakening Revival in days before railways had spread over the country, and means of locomotion were scarce and uncomfortable, and roads bad. " Puffing Billy," as our earliest locomotive was named, it will be remembered, did not make its appearance until 1813, and many years elapsed before Stephenson's plans materialised. Yet obstacles were overcome by men who " scorned delights and lived laborious days." Hardly a corner of England remained outside the influence of those times of refreshing. In Haworth, in Yorkshire, famed in after years as the home of the Brontë family, William Grimshaw won a whole country-side from practical heathenism to sober Godliness. Men walked forty miles on a Sunday to attend the ministry of this apostolic man. He found a church with twelve communicants ; in a few years more than twelve hundred approached the Lord's table on a single Sunday.

To take another example. In Truro, in Cornwall, then a small town of sixteen hundred inhabitants, Samuel Walker, a young man of good family, graceful manners and address, had been placed as curate-in-charge by an absentee rector. Walker was fond of dancing, cards and gay company, but performed his duties in church with regularity and decorum. To spiritual religion he was a stranger until he was brought into contact with the master of Truro Grammar School, said to be the first Evangelical Churchman the county furnished. From him Walker learned the meaning of the Gospel. He began to preach justification by Faith as set forth in Hooker's great sermon, and followed it up by a life of intense devotion and unworldliness. The formal worshippers were startled and angry, but the church soon filled, conversions followed, communicants increased, and before many years had passed Truro became one of the most religious towns in England. It was said that during the hour of service on Sunday morning a cannon might be fired down the street and no one hit. The town was at prayer.

In other parts of the country there were men like Scott, the Commentator, to whom Cardinal Newman owed his soul; Toplady, author of "Rock of Ages"; John Newton, curate of Olney; Fletcher of Madley, the Saint of the movement; Thomas Adam, the Pascal of Evangelicalism, whose "Private thoughts on Religion" John Stuart Mill lingered over with fondness, reading it again and again. This period was for England the flowering time of true spiritual religion. Never had the country such a visitation before, never such a visitation since. We have seen how it was received by the people; something may now be said of its reception by the Church and the Church authorities. There did not fail, in the worst days of the later Stuarts and in the duller period of the Revolution and the Georges, a succession of sober, conscientious churchmen who, as pointed out by Mr. Wakeman in his somewhat romantic description of those times,[1] maintained a high standard of life in their parishes. Such men would fall under the description, in our day, of " Old-fashioned high-Churchmen." It must

---

[1] " History of the Church of England."

be confessed that this class, while not actively opposing, looked with coldness and suspicion on the whole Evangelical movement, and in a quiet way used their influence to suppress it and restrain its leaders. They lived in a perpetual fear of enthusiasm. On the other hand, some of the bishops were actively hostile. Lavington, bishop of Exeter, made frequent attempts to silence Walker of Truro, anticipating one of his great successors, Henry Philpotts, who prohibited deputations from the Church Missionary Society entering his diocese. The Archbishop of York was called on to deal with Grimshaw of Haworth, and actually came in person to his parish to reprove him, but ended by blessing him when he saw the fruits of his faithful ministry. If the Evangelicals won their way to the hearts of the people it must be confessed that it was not due to Episcopal favour, or to encouragement from the general body of the clergy. At the same time it would not be just to blame the Church authorities unduly for their caution. The old order rarely changes in any department of life without awakening fears and anxieties, and if the English Episcopate has at times given occasion to critics to censure it as *semper pavidus*, it might very easily have exposed itself to something worse.

It may surprise those who speak of Evangelicals as Low Churchmen to learn that it was from the Low Churchmen of those times the most active opposition to the Revival came. The Evangelicals could never at any time be properly described by this term. Their motto throughout has been " Spiritual men for spiritual work," and whatever the Low

Churchman may have been, spiritual he was not. He ate, he drank, he hunted, he swore, his Church was often filthy, his surplice little better, he rattled through the service as fast as he cleared fences in the hunting field. Though sometimes of a kindly disposition and generous to the poor, he was a good fellow rather than a good man, and the one thing he seemed most unfitted for was the fulfilment of his ordination vow to search for Christ's sheep that are scattered abroad.

Grimshaw before his conversion was a type, though not an extreme type, of the Low Church parson, and here is a description of him : " He read prayers and a sermon once every Sunday. He refrained as much as possible from gross swearing unless in suitable company, and when he got drunk, would take care to sleep it out before he came home. He was a huntsman, a fisherman, a first rate card player, anything but a herald of the Cross." [1]   The Grimshaw of Evangelicalism, com-pared with this, was literally a new creation. It was men of this description who suborned ruffians to disturb Evangelical assemblies and ill-use the preachers. Truly, if a great door and effectual was opened to the Evangelicals, there were many adversaries.

Much as we admire the later Puritans for such works as are here glanced at, truth obliges us to admit that they did not make the most of their opportun-ities. At one time they were strong enough to have purged the English drama and sweetened

---

[1] Balleine, " History of the Evangelical Party," p. 65.

the fount of literature ; and possibly the greatest
mistake they ever made was their wholesale condemnation of both.   To many minds the reform
of the Stage is a more urgent question, in its bearing on public morals, than the reform of the Church.
Men possessed of the congenial godliness of Hutchinson, the broad sanity of Sir Thomas Browne, the
reasonableness and sanctified worldly wisdom of
Whitelock, might have undertaken the task, but
they had few successors.   Thus Puritanism, like
some of the religious orders, withdrew into itself,
and contented itself with its great works of Evangelisation and Philanthropy and Social Reform.
This was a grievous error of judgment, for it left
the amusements of the people and popular fiction
in the hands of those whose aims were rarely high,
and whose morals were often low.

This is the more astonishing when we consider
that there was nothing ungenial in the characters
of men like Wilberforce and Thornton.   They may
not have looked on mankind in general with such
a kindly eye as that of Sir Thomas Browne, or the
American Puritan poet who wrote: —

"In human nature still I find more good than ill ;"

but they were no "kill-joys." Sydney Smith
made fine play with their jovial gatherings and
high festivities.   Amongst the Evangelical clergy
of the sternest Puritan type in those days must be
reckoned John Newton, curate of Olney, to whose
alleged gloomy views of human nature the depres-
sion of spirits from which Cowper often suffered
has been put down.   But Newton's admirers in

our day, while admitting his strong Calvinistic
bent, have made out a good case for him as a cheerful companion in private life, where his high spirits
acted like a tonic on his friends and his ministry
did much more to heal than to aggravate Cowper's
mental infirmity. Indeed, it would be hard to
believe that the man who embellished one of his
hymns with a line so unusual in Church compo-
sitions as

"We hope to die shouting 'the Lord will provide.'"

was void of humour in the pulpit or out of it. On
the other hand, as regards Cowper himself, two
interesting and hitherto unpublished letters written
by him in 1789, furnished recently to the *Spectator* by the president of Haverford College,
Pennsylvania, reveal such a delicate sense of
humour in Cowper as to lead one to believe
that "John Gilpin" gives us a better clue
to his mind than those writers who present him as
one whose cheerfulness had been destroyed by his
religion. It would be more correct to say that,
in his case at least, Calvinism had a very wholesome
effect.

There was nothing therefore in Puritanism itself,
nor in the character of its advocates, which pre-
cluded the latter from taking an active part in
purifying and elevating the pastimes and recreations of the country ; and that they failed to do
so must ever be regarded as a serious omission of
duty on their part.

CHAPTER XIX

WE have seen how Cromwell favoured the work of evangelising the heathen and the Jew, and the restoration of the latter to Palestine, his founding of the Society for the Propagation of the Gospel, afterwards taken over and reconstituted by the Church of England, his interest in education and its diffusion throughout the country. In all of these matters the Evangelicals faithfully upheld the Puritan tradition. Nothing can be farther from the truth than the aspersion that they sought only the salvation of their own souls. In one of his letters Wilberforce, who was admonished not to neglect his soul in the great work he had in hand, declares that for weeks he had not even thought whether he had had a soul. This by no means implied that he had relinquished his accustomed devotions ; but the miseries of his fellow-creatures in slavery so oppressed him that self was lost sight of in the all-absorbing effort to win the nation to a right understanding of its duty.

Freedom, religious and political, we have frequently observed, was the essential note of Puritanism and to this the Protector had applied himself with energy. If popery and prelacy did not share in its benefits, sufficient political reasons existed, as we have seen, for their exclusion. The historian who gives the fact and omits the explanation is guilty of a *suppressio veri*; a too common fault with the partisan. But if this principle be carried to its logical conclusion the whole world must be made free, and the two aspects of freedom must either proceed *pari passu* or the one inevitably follow the other; that is to say, the reception of a gospel which gives men the highest form of liberty —" If the Son shall make you free ye shall be free indeed"—must be accompanied or followed by a social freedom recognising the brotherhood of Christians and securely safeguarding the rights of individuals; circumstances of course determining the measure and extent of its application; in fullest measure where the people are ripe for it, more gradually and cautiously where they are not sufficiently advanced to make wise use of it. Puritan America gave voice to these ideas in the popular war-song of the States, the Marseillaise of the Northern army :

" In the beauty of the lilies Christ was born across the sea,
  With a glory in His bosom that transfigures you and me.
  As He died to make men holy, let us live to make men free,
  For God is marching on."

Such sentiments are the natural fruits of Puritanism, and can no more fail to arise from its teaching than the flower can help blooming, or the rivers help running to the sea. The leading organ of the English Press writes in our day, "In the crisis through which the liberties of the world have lately passed Puritanism has been justified of her children.

Was it not the prime motive that brought the descendants of the men who sailed in the *Mayflower* back to Europe to defend those very principles and liberties for which Cromwell fought and for which the Pilgrim Fathers cast their bread and their lives upon the broad waters of the Atlantic ? "[1] As we follow the course of the stream, watching with interest its increase, we come to a new aspect of Puritanism, yet with principles unchanged.

Spiritual freedom in its highest aspects and civil rights for every "child of Adam's race" was the goal aimed at by the Evangelical party in the English Church as truly as by Cromwell. A small group of laymen, well-born, highly educated, skilled in affairs, devout and resolute, found themselves almost fortuitously assembled in the town of Clapham, late in the eighteenth century. They were deeply attached to Evangelical principles and were thereby brought into contact with several clergymen holding similar views.

To these men it is due that Christianity has touched every nation under heaven, that Christian civilisation has in many countries displaced grossest barbarism and cannibalism, and that the darkest stain on England's reputation has been wiped out for ever. If the Roundheads sowed the seed, the Evangelicals of the eighteenth and nineteenth centuries reaped much of the fruit. Cromwell viewed, like Moses, the Promised Land, it remained for a later race of Puritans to cross the Jordan.

We shall confine ourselves for the present to a

The Times, August 2nd, 1919.

brief notice of Puritan evangelism abroad and at home, reserving the consideration of its political undertakings for a future chapter. The overseas work of the English Church was so feeble and ineffective in those days as to be scarcely worthy of notice, but the nonconforming Puritan churches were active, as well as Danish and Moravian missionaries.[1] The Methodist Church had taken up work amongst the West Indian negroes, and the single-hearted Carey had gone to India under the auspices of the Baptist Missionary Society; the London Missionary Society—at first undenominational in character, afterwards the recognised missionary society of the Congregational Church —commenced its great work amongst the South Sea islanders in the year 1795; and the Scottish Presbyterians almost immediately after launched two societies for the evangelising of the heathen. In 1799 the Eclectic Society—a body composed of the London Evangelical clergy, a few Evangelical laymen, and two dissenting ministers—began seriously to face the question of a definite work amongst the people of the East; and on April the 12th of the same year, at a meeting held in the Castle and Falcon Hotel, Aldersgate Street, the Church Missionary Society was founded. Its beginnings were small and unpropitious, but it was destined to become the greatest Protestant missionary society in the world. Up to this time the English Church possessed no organisation for work of this character. The Society for Promoting

---

[1] Balleine, " History of the Evangelical Party," Chap. VI.

Christian Knowledge gave a grant to a Lutheran mission in India ; the Society for the Propagation of the Gospel confined its labours to our fellow-subjects overseas, while neither society would have any dealings with Evangelicals, many of their members going so far as to write and speak against them. Here, then, we have on the one hand the National Church, as represented by its highest officials, apathetic regarding the Church's primary duty, and on the other, English Puritanism of almost every phase sending forth evangelists to the ends of the earth—Methodists, Baptists, Presbyterians, Independents and Evangelical Churchmen making up this goodly fellowship of the Prophets. The effect of these missionary enterprises on thoughtful and devout minds amongst the English high-Churchmen of those days cannot be fairly estimated, but we may assume that it was considerable ; for a day came when the noble example set by the Evangelicals stirred their brethren of other parties into activity and caused them to abound in works of faith and labours of love in heathen and Moslem lands. In process of time Puritan America also sent its missionary army into the field. A comparison of the English Church of to-day with what it was when Sydney Smith wrote of " the Clapham Sect," will show clearly that the Evangelical party has not only influenced but completely revolution-ised Christian thought in England on this subject. To be " interested in missions " in Sydney Smith's day was to be suspected as a " peculiar " ; it was in fact the mark of a despised Evangelical ; to be

indifferent in our day is to stand outside the main
current of Church life. We do not know whether
Charles Dickens meant to satirise foreign missions,
in his character of Mrs. Jellaby, who could see
nothing nearer than Africa. Nineteenth century
novelists—Thackeray and Besant for instance—
had little to say in favour either of the work or the
workers ; and Disraeli, in " Sybil," asks petulantly
could not one missionary be spared from Tahiti to
minister to the degraded inhabitants of Wodgate ?
Such criticisms were both ignorant and unjust.
England, with a population of eleven millions, had
nearly fifteen thousand clergy, with church build-
ings and endowments, besides many thousands of
dissenting ministers, while along the coast of West
Africa, the Sudan, and from Mozambique to the
Nile, not a single herald of the Cross could be found
telling the story of redeeming love to the millions
of natives, who were as much entitled to it as the
cynical novelist or our Hebrew prime minister.
The fact is, England had workers enough to cover
the land, but England and its Church were asleep,
and it was the men who arose to awake them out
of sleep to whom the lash of the critic was applied.
Very soon, however, these energetic Evangelicals
proved that they had other thoughts, and room in
their hearts for other interests, than those of Africa
and the East. If the work of Wesley and Whitfield
was not to die out, much remained to be done at
home. There were many practical heathens still
to be found in English parishes ; in our sweetest
villages and quietest hamlets, so pleasing in out-

ward appearance, ignorance of the most elementary
Christianity prevailed and moral standards were
very low. In the coarse language of the time, " a
base child " often signified in the parish register
the origin of a boy or girl brought for baptism to
the Church, a ceremony generally regarded, where
it was observed, as a sort of magical charm. In
many parts of the country rural scenery was passing, and huge factories, blazing furnaces and black
mining villages taking its place. To meet the
spiritual needs created by such altered circumstances, the Evangelicals founded the Church
Pastoral Aid Society, as at an earlier period they
had founded the Religious Tract Society, the one
to send more clergymen and duly accredited laymen
to minister to the growing population, the other
to provide healthy religious and moral reading in
language suited to its capacity. But probably the
most remarkable auxiliary of the Christian Church
established in that or in any age, was the British
and Foreign Bible Society ; for that society not
only became in time the friend of all the Christian
churches and Christian missions in the world,
providing the scriptures to them in every known
and every newly discovered language, but con-
sciously or unconsciously it was the first definite
step towards the reunion of the Protestant
churches of the world. In its committee room
and on its platform meet all denominations of
Protestant Christians, and for the time lose the
consciousness of their denominations in the large
catholicity of this great society, whose achieve-

ments, reaching over one complete century, are as near an approach to the miraculous as anything we are ever likely to see.

Cromwell's interest in the Jew has been surpassed by the friends of the London Society for Promoting Christianity amongst the Jews, another product of those times and of the Church Evangelicals. Its task is by no means a light one, but it is one that could not be neglected by a body of Christians who guide their lives and activities by the Scriptures. Its success has been notable. Like almost all the efforts of this party, it has on more than one occasion been fiercely attacked by a well-meaning but reactionary section of English ecclesiastics, but in every case it has been proved to have acted and taught in loyal conformity to English Church standards. To meet the call of Newfoundland and WesternAustralia, where our colonists were slipping, almost imperceptibly, into a life closely allied to barbarism, an appeal was made to the Church at home without success. In the case of Australia the reply of the venerable Society for the Propagation of the Gospel was : " We have not the means and we have not the men." There was nothing for it but that the Evangelicals should once more step into the breach, and this they did with such vigour that Australia and Canada reap to-day the fruit of their sacrifice, while the principal places of resort on the Continent of Europe are provided with churches and chaplains, some of the latter occupying permanent posts, for the purpose of ministering the Christian religion to English - speaking residents and

visitors according to the usage of the English
Church.

Itineration at home had shown Wesley and the
Evangelicals the spiritual state of England. Life
abroad had revealed to men like Zachary Macaulay
and Grant the condition of the heathen; and here
we see, created by a despised, suspected and much-
misrepresented party a vast network of organisation, instinct with spiritual power, covering the
land of England and reaching to remotest parts
of the globe; organisations which sought only the
salvation of men's souls and the glory of God.
From the point of view of Church law and order, it
was indeed a bitter irony of fate that led the rulers
of the Church to look with coldness on this party
and to discourage many of its enterprises. The
Church papers denounced the Pastoral Aid Society;
the Bishop of Exeter, who become noteworthy for
his opposition to the Church Missionary Society's
agents, now pronounces the proposals of this home
agency to be "contrary to the practice of all
Christian antiquity . . . pregnant with mischief
and perils of the gravest kind." The Bishop of
London was equally unsympathetic. A scheme for
associating the English Church and the Lutheran
in the provision of a bishop for Jerusalem set the
pens of Pusey and Newman in motion, declaring
Lutheranism and Calvinism to be heresies condemned by the Catholic Church. Newman, who
at an earlier period had acted as an honorary
correspondent at Oxford for the Church Missionary Society, put out a suggestion about the
year 1830 that the High Church party should

capture it by swamping the committee with their
men. Of course the plot would have failed, but
it is greatly to their honour that the old High Church
party never made the attempt. These few facts
are mentioned in order to show to what extent the
Puritans of the later time suffered the slings and
arrows of fortune; for let it be remembered that
the Evangelical Churchmen of this period were
warmly attached to their church, loyal and submissive to those set over them, and faithful ex-
ponents of the Church's doctrine as set forth in the
Prayer Book, Articles and Homilies.

The question arises, would they have fared
better had they enjoyed the favour and patronage
of the great? There can be little doubt that they
throve well on persecution, if we may apply such
a term to the treatment they received. If doors
were closed to them in England, those of Africa
and the East were wide open. If bishoprics and
canonries did not fall to them, humble spheres of
widest usefulness offered on many hands. Trust
patronage sprang up, and sent them into important parishes; private patrons took notice of
them; and by such means and the employment
of lay agents and humble Scripture readers, tract
distributors and Bible colporteurs, the land was
filled with their message. So deep was the impression made in those times that in our day more
than eighty years after the rise of Tractarianism,
which has captured four-fifths of the English
clergy, the country remains Puritan at heart.

What is an almost equally interesting fact is the
adoption one by one of the denounced schemes

and methods of the party by their former critics. Foreign missions, home missions, lay work, parochial missions, open-air preaching, Sunday schools, popular hymns, temperance societies, all find their place in active High Church parishes. The Jerusalem bishopric no longer excites anger, and the Church Missionary Society enjoys a large measure of Episcopal favour. The methods resorted to by the early Evangelicals to arouse England from spiritual slumber are now the common possession of all parties.

Coming down to the present time, we have, as proof of the continued vitality of the party, a work of surpassing merit and usefulness in the various missions to Seamen, missions which aim at the preservation of men's souls and bodies in hundreds of well-managed Sailors' institutes and comely mission churches. Here the seaman is at home and free. Here he can read his paper, smoke his pipe, play his game, write his letter, sing his song, and spin his yarn, no man forbidding him. When he presents himself at the sailors' church, no punctilious verger stands, like the flaming cherubim at the portals of Eden, to warn him off the sacred ground of the appropriated pew. When his vessel lies at anchor in the roadstead a mission schooner finds him out, and brings him temporal and spiritual comforts. Not the least of the many merciful services rendered him by his mission friends is the method adopted by the Board of Trade, at the instance of these missions, of transmitting his wages to his home on his arrival in port. The sailor, being a frail child of dust, rarely succeeded in running the gauntlet of the grog-shop, and the dancing saloon, and the wiles of the poor painted bawds, which welcomed him at the end of every voyage and cast him off when the last coin was spent. Work of a similar character is carried on amongst men of the Royal Navy, inaugurated by the late Agnes Weston, through whose agency two magnificent palaces, appropriately named " Sailors' Rests," have been set up, one in Portsmouth and the other in Devonport. The Evangelicals have given us many noble daughters whose work at home and in mission fields overseas is beyond praise. They would all assign a special niche in the temple of fame to this great-hearted sister who gave her life, her love, her all to the British Blue Jackets. The seaports of England, once scenes of indescribable vice and violence, are, through these agencies, become safe and peaceful places—for the peacefully disposed.

But time would fail us to mention in detail the many works of mercy which this party has taken in hand, sometimes by a society, sometimes by " a free lance," for England's welfare. Our purpose is to show what few will dispute, that our modern Puritan, in nearly every case, led the way. Sunday schools, ragged schools, night schools, working-men's clubs, friendly societies, rescue work, boys' and girls' orphan and other homes, all owe their origin, or their revival, to some kind Puritan heart, moved with pity at the condition of his neglected neighbours. The world cannot furnish a more romantic story of philanthropy than the story of Dr. Barnardo's Homes in Stepney Causeway and Ilford. The accidental meeting of a young medical student and a ragged child—homeless, outcast, hungry, ignorant—mere flotsam and jetsam on the restless sea of life, to be picked up or left to drift as fate or Providence might determine, resulted in the founding of those homes, from which tens of thousands are gone forth into the world to enrich it with their labour and their example. The Army, the Navy, the ministry of Christian churches, the farms and ranches of Canada and Australia, are yearly receiving their share of the young life of England, rescued, saved, humanised, Christianised, through this agency. Truly, Puritanism is still a force in the world, when miracles of this sort are wrought through its means. And its zeal has provoked very many. Other men and women, not calling themselves Puritan—far removed, in fact, therefrom—impressed by the need, and encouraged by Puritan successes, have now taken their place in the crusade of philanthropy, not in rivalry, but in a spirit of friendly emulation. Churchmen and Dissenters closed their ranks against a common danger in the reign of James II., as they had done when the plague was carrying off its thousands daily in 1646. Puritan and High Churchmen, in this our day, are one in their desire to rescue the submerged child-life of England, and give it a chance of rational and useful existence.

CHAPTER XX

THE abolition of the Slave Trade has been pronounced by a reliable English historian to be " one
of the three or four perfectly virtuous acts recorded
in the History of Nations." [1]

It was, in the opinion of Overton, the work of
Evangelicalism as much as of Evangelicals. Holding the religious views of their party, they felt
that this burden was laid on them, and, being
what they were, they needs must do what they
did. The whole human race had been redeemed, not merely a part of it, by the passion of
its incarnate Lord ; man, the sum total man, was
the object of the Divine Compassion ; the bodies
of men as well as their souls. It was not, therefore,
possible that men and women who had put their
hand to re-making England by means of purer
literature, preaching, visiting, voluntary schools,
prison and factory reform, and who were sending
missionaries to heathen lands, could tolerate a
state of things in West India which the public
conscience condemned in England. Humanity is
not a geographical idea. The Gospel is a great
leveller, an exalter if you will ; if it were wrong

Lecky, " European Morals," vol. I. p. 160.

to whip English boys and girls until weals rose
and blood streamed from their backs, and then
to aggravate their pains by shaking pepper into
their wounds, it could not be just to inflict such
tortures on negroes. If raids on English villages
were a thing inconceivable, and no one had power
to drag men, women and children in chains to
the coast and huddle them together on filthy
slave-ships, to be carried over sea and sold into
slavery for work on sugar plantations, was it
possible to sanction such a system in our colonies ?
The cruelties, the inhumanities, the barbarities of
the plantations had converted "one quarter of
the earth into the nearest possible resemblance of
what we conceive of hell." [1] The trade degraded
the planter, dishonoured England, and made the
Gospel a mockery, and the preachers who favoured
the trade a race of hypocrites, for by what other
name can we describe the man who proclaims with
St. Paul the equal rights of all races within the
Christian fold, and yet, while holding the English
child free, regards the negro child as a chattel to
be sold and bought in the market-place ? Men
into whose souls these facts had burned were now
found in the British Parliament, and were faced
with the opposition, not of mere "worldlings,"
of whom the House had a sufficiency, but of many
who regarded themselves as exemplary Christians,
some of them even professing the Evangelical
principles from which the handful of Abolitionists
drew their arguments and their inspiration. The
battle was a long one, but the Clapham sect had

Stephens' Essay, " The Clapham Sect."

nailed the colours to the mast and never dreamt
of surrender.   In vain did merchants, ship-owners,
planters and financiers raise the cry that England
would be ruined, the colonies lost, the negroes rise
and murder their masters.   In vain did the dull,
unimaginative king fume at the pious gentlemen
of Clapham, as a danger to the State and the
advance-guard of a reign of terror, while the
official classes poured scorn on the humanity-
mongers.   In vain did Nelson from the *Victory*
launch his voice "against the damnable doctrine
of Wilberforce and his hypocritical allies."   Possibly from the beginning the advocates of slavery
knew the cause was doomed.   For one thing it
was indefensible ; for another the men who
declared war on it were known to be in the House
of Commons for that purpose, and no other.   Place,
privilege, reputation, counted for nothing with
them.   The cause of righteousness was everything.
No abler or more eloquent member adorned the
Parliament of 1787 than Wilberforce, who first
took up the subject in that year.   His position in
society and his high character commanded the
respect and attention of his strongest opponents ;
and he had the countenance of one member whose
influence might fairly be weighed against the
whole opposition.   Pitt was on his side.   For
twenty years the struggle went on, and we cannot
even now, with diaries and letters in abundance
to consult, form a correct estimate of the patience,
the hopes, the endurance, the persistency of the
brave band who seemed to have made up their
minds, like William of Orange, "to die in the last

dyke " rather than accept defeat.   The holding of
meetings for informing and influencing public
opinion, the writing and issuing of pamphlets;
committees, petitions, deputations, interviews, all-
night sittings of workers, such are some of the
labours recorded of those strenuous times.   Eleven
times the bill was defeated; But at last came
victory;   283 votes for it and only 16 against.
For men whose minds are set on righteousness
and jealous for England's good name, it was a
prouder day than Trafalgar or Waterloo.   This
was in 1807; but six and twenty years later,
after a struggle of ten years, another Bill was
passed through Parliament by a younger generation of Evangelicals, headed by Fowell Buxton,
to complete the Act of 1807; for although the
earlier measure had abolished the slave trade,
it had not abolished slavery; the unhappy negroes
who were on the plantations had to remain there
until death gave them release.   Exeter Hall has
often been held up to derision, but it uttered a
voice at this time, loud and strong enough to shake
the Government of the day, before which the
opposition gave way.   Slavery was declared to be
henceforth unlawful in any British possession;
a sum of twenty millions was voted as compensa-
tion to the planters; Puritanism had at last wiped
out the reproach.   This was by no means a party
victory.   Fowell Buxton was a Whig.   The
Quakers and Methodists who in and outside the
House supported him were mostly Whigs.   Ashley
and the Church Evangelicals were Tories.   But
they were all one in the great purpose which united

them, and unity insured success. The wholesome effect of these titanic struggles in the cause of humanity on political thought was not confined to England. Puritan America felt its conscience touched by it, and not the least important result of the American Civil War of 1861-4 was the freeing of the whole slave population of the States ; young America could not withhold what old England granted, the daughter must follow the footsteps of the mother who gave her birth. No stronger proof could be furnished, or need be asked, than this overthrow of slavery, of the strength and the persistency of the life of Puritanism. The two great Puritan nations of the world step to the front, giving a lead to all civilised peoples in the matter of their duty towards their less favoured brethren. " There was a time," writes Carlyle, " when Puritanism was despicable, laughable ; but nobody can laugh at it now. Puritanism has got weapons and sinews ; it has firearms, war navies ; it has cunning in its ten fingers, strength in its right arm ; it can steer ships, fell forests, remove mountains ; it is one of the strongest things under this sun at present." [1]

A few words may here be added on America's part in this most Christian act of emancipation. It cost that nation much to set its slaves free ; far more than it cost us to free ours. But it was done, and done without ostentation. Nothing is more noble in the life of Lincoln—in a life which was all noble—than the simple, honest way in

---

[1] Essay, "Hero Worship," Vol. VI. p. 133.

which he declares that he did not make war to put down slavery. That was not his objective. He drew the sword reluctantly, there was no other way, for the unity and consolidation of his country ; and he will not seek popularity with sentimentalists and humanitarians all the world over by pretending another and less interested motive. Had he done so, there can be no doubt that sympathy would have flowed to him from many a quarter where, through misunderstanding, it was withheld ; but the clean, truthful soul of the man could not stoop to this. The slavery question came up, but it was subsidiary, and Lincoln and the nation met it in the right spirit. The price was heavy, and it was paid, and is still paying, in other than coin of the Republic. Nevertheless, be the price what it may, America's hands and ours are now clean in this matter.

If we would ask whence came the motive which set all those great souls to work in this crusade of liberty ? Why did they not let well enough alone ? Slavery was profitable ; the colonies were enriching the mother country; the children of Ham were by destiny and divine decree the servants of the white races—treat them a little more mercifully and all will be well. Many good men reasoned in this fashion. Why did not such reasoning prevail ? The answer is that Puritanism made it impossible. The Bible, and the Puritan Church and Meeting House, supplied the motive power that silenced the advocates of slavery and utterly destroyed the hateful thing itself. Half measures were not good enough for men who had

learned that " the judgments of the Lord are true
and righteous altogether."

In dealing with the Evangelicals as politicians
we are brought down to recent times. This
Puritan with his creed of righteousness is a persistent fellow, and a most troublesome politician·
What scandal has he not unearthed ; what injustice has he not exposed ? Three matters at
least have greatly troubled him in our day : the
Native races, the Drink traffic, and Opium. These
questions in the House of Commons have been
almost the exclusive property of Evangelical
Churchmen, Quakers, and other devout Nonconformists. Help has been given from other
quarters, but these have led the way.

Outside the House information was obtained by
the Aborigines Protection Society and the Anti-
Slavery Society, as to the treatment of native races
by Europeans, and the question of their rights was
frequently raised in the Commons by the two
Fowlers, the one a Quaker and a Liberal, the other
an Evangelical Churchman and a Tory, who were
kept supplied with facts by the two societies named.
Owing to the representations of these members,
and others who sympathised with them, much
relief came to the Maoris in New Zealand and the
black races in Africa. The humanitarian party
naturally came into great disfavour with the Boer
population in South Africa, who resented the
exposure of their evil deeds before the British
Parliament. Moffat and Livingstone had given
anything but a pleasant impression of the attitude
of the Boer settlers towards the native tribes in

their vicinity—an attitude illustrated by a typical incident in the missionary records of those times. A missionary had hospitality offered him at the farm of a prosperous Boer, who made no small profession of his piety. The guest, on being asked to conduct family prayers before retiring, asked that "the boys" might be called in to join in worship. "Call in the boys!" exclaimed the master in wrath; "call in the dogs!" No Kaffir Christian shared in that service. The master's association of him with his dogs fairly indicates the general feeling of the average Boer towards the Black, in the days before the South African War. The Puritan Party in the House of Commons, Evangelicals of the strictest type, found a strange ally at this time in the heterodox Bishop of Natal, Dr. Colenso. If righteousness and mercy should be weighed against orthodoxy in that high court from which there is no appeal, the friends of Colenso need not tremble for his fate; more than any other bishop that ever served the Church in South Africa he proved himself the faithful, disinterested friend of the native tribes.

It is not likely that under any treatment the negro will ever reach the standard of the white man, but these Puritan reformers have compelled white men to regard him as a human being and a fellow-heir of the Kingdom of God. Much more follows. The Church Missionary Society has prevailed to raise two negroes and a Hindu to the Episcopate; while the South American Missionary Society, another offspring of Puritanism, has succeeded in humanising, civilising, and in part Christianising

the inhabitants of Tierra del Fuego; a task pronounced to be impossible by Professor Darwin,
and its successful accomplishment "the story of
the magician's wand." Of such stout stuff were
these Evangelicals made they could "laugh at
impossibilities and say it shall be done."

Opium and Alcohol were known to be powerful
drugs; a blessing in the hands of a skilful physician,
a curse when sold indiscriminately to pander to a
debased appetite; and upon this indiscriminate
manufacture and sale the party made relentless
war. Missionaries pictured the opium dens of
China, with their thousands of lost souls, wills
destroyed, nightly steeped in exquisite stupor.
In large measure Christian England, having forced
opium for the sake of profit upon China, was
responsible for this. Again the voice of the Quaker
was raised in Parliament. England's patronage
of this scourge must cease; and cease it did.
There was no need to visit China and India in
order to picture the evils of alcohol; they lay all
around us. Seven-tenths of the diseases of a great
London hospital, Sir Andrew Clark declared, were
traceable to the abuse of this drug. Disease,
however, represented but a small portion of the
evil: vice, crime, neglected and impoverished
homes, starving children, reared in squalor and
ignorance, and a thousand other fruits of this
trade, menaced the character and even the very
existence of the nation. By legislation and by
moral suasion, at first mainly promoted by Nonconformists, it was sought to save the country from
itself. Societies were formed; lecturers were sent

all over the land ; temperance tracts flooded towns, villages, hamlets ; all the churches, including the Roman, joined in the campaign of enlightenment and warning.   It was in returning from a temperance demonstration in Exeter Hall that one of the most interesting incidents in the late Cardinal Manning's life occurred.   Passing a group of Salvationist singers and preachers, he lowered the window of his cab and, reaching out his hand, solemnly gave them his blessing.   To the surprised question of his nephew, who had asked how he could reconcile the act with his profession, he quietly replied, as he raised the window : " I do not try to reconcile it.   I only know these poor people, with such knowledge as they have, are trying to make known in these vile streets the only Name by which men can be saved ; and I hope it will come right somehow."   The incident serves to show that the temperance movement, over and above its direct effects, was promoting effects of another kind : setting many of the idle rich to work, drawing Christian churches together, and softening political animosities amongst men of good will.   Sir Wilfred Lawson for many years led the attack on the Trade in the House of Commons. He was, in his day, a Radical of Radicals, yet the diary of a strong Tory, who sympathised with his temperance efforts, contained the remark, after a general election : " Lawson is returned again.   I am glad he is in."

The Temperance Party has not yet achieved its purpose, but it has won victories its founders little thought of.   It has created a healthy public

opinion ; it has made thousands of converts ; it
has revolutionised the habits of the respectable
middle classes ; and although its Parliamentary
triumphs have been scanty, owing to powerful
trade interests in both political parties, it has
succeeded in promoting some useful legislation,
and is hopeful that more may follow.   In thinking
over these things it would be ungrateful to forget
the small group of resolute, determined men, all
of them with blood and traditions of the old
Puritans in them, and especially " the men of
Preston," who, amidst derision and misrepresentation, set their minds on making a sober England,
and were first in pointing the way to its attainment.

CHAPTER XXI

PURITANISM AND THE UNIVERSITIES

THE Universities of a country should represent its highest thinking. There we may look for the men who will influence the thought of the nation and become the builders or the architects of its institutions, repairing or remaking the old, and providing, as the time calls for them, the new. It is one of the capital errors of a section of that political party in England which appropriates the title of "Labour" that the wealth of the country is created solely by men's hands. Brains and capital are even more necessary to such ends than hand-labour; and the man who has thought to give, and gives it freely, is as much a labourer as he who wields a pick, or wheels a barrow, or guides a plough. Again, the distribution of wealth is not of less importance than the acquiring of it. Wise spending may be a more difficult art to learn than that easy earning that is grown so common, and which often enough is a rough-and-ready sort of business. Then in the case of a nation like England, having possessions in every quarter of the globe, magistrates, judges, governors, proconsuls are a necessity; and however ready we may be to put up with indifferent men in Parliament, we can run no risks in our civil, consular, and diplomatic services. For these the highest intelligence, knowledge, and character the country can provide must be forthcoming. " I believe in brains," was the saying of an old soldier who had received much hurt from the brainless. And yet this is not enough. Brains must be trained, disciplined, informed, made orderly, before they can be employed usefully. It is from the undisciplined brain anarchy usually springs. The wisdom of the Greeks provided for the training of both mind and body ; and here we see the prime use and necessity of the University.

The well-known aphorism " Who drives fat oxen should himself be fat," may be adapted to the heads of our seats of learning in the form : " Who disciplines others should himself be disciplined." We cannot expect a college to turn out men of character and wisdom unless the members of its teaching staff exhibit these qualities in themselves. What then was the character of our Universities before the Puritans took possession of them ? What was it when Puritanism was expelled from them ? Was the influence of the party good or bad, and has it left any permanent mark on these institutions ?

These questions must now engage our attention for a short time. The delightful Pepys, who loved a well-paid Government post, grand company, and good wine, as much as he loved his fine dinner on " a dish of marrow bones ; a leg of mutton ; a loin of veal ; a dish of fowl, three pullets, and a dozen larks all in a dish ; a great tart, a neat's tongue ; a dish of anchovies ; a dish of prawns and cheese " ; is, in his diary, the most truthful of men. He is utterly worldly ; but a more frank and simple-minded worldling never existed. Mr. Herring's lazy, poor sermon, and the buckles on Samuel Pepys's shoes, are matters of equal importance. The evidence of a man who pours himself out in this way, without reflection, may be trusted. Hear what he says, then, of one of our Universities, on the verge of the Restoration, when Puritanism was, for the time, on its last legs at Cambridge : " We two came to Cambridge by eight o'clock in the morning. I went to Magdalene College to Mr. Hill, with whom I found Mr. Zanchy, Burton and Hollins, and took leave on promise to sup with them. To the Three Tuns, where we drank pretty hard and many healths to the King (Charles II.), &c. : then we broke up, and I and Mr. Zanchy went to Magdalene College, where a very handsome supper at Mr. Hill's chambers, I suppose upon a club among them, where I could find that there was nothing at all left of the old preciseness in their discourse, specially on Saturday nights. And Mr. Zanchy told me that there was no such thing among them now-a-days at any time."[1]

Nothing at all left of the old preciseness ; no such thing among them now-a-days at any time ! Truly coming events were casting their shadows before them. From Pepys we may turn to Stoughton, whose sketch of " Oxford under

---

[1] Pepys's Diary, February 23rd, 1659.

Owen,"[1] though the work of an advocate, will be
found quite trustworthy as regards facts. Stoughton relies chiefly on Wood's "Annals of the
University," and Peck's "Desiderata Curiosa" :
the former no friend of Puritanism. It will be
remembered that Oxford was for a long period
during the Civil War the headquarters of the king ;
the University, in fact, became a garrison, the
gownsmen steel-helmeted soldiers, with the stride,
the swagger, and, most willingly it must be confessed, the habits of the cavalier. In the June of
1646 Oxford resistance to Fairfax came to an end,
the men of the surrendered garrison, three thousand
in number, marched out under arms along the
road to Shotover Hill, and the Puritan forces
marching in occupied the town and the colleges.
They found the seat of Minerva a desolation.
The schools had been turned into granaries, the
colleges into barracks, the butteries into shops for
the sale of ale and beer to the King's Army. Build-
ings had fallen into decay ; Gothic halls and
chambers were defaced and spoiled by a rude
soldiery. Books had disappeared ; college plate
had been melted down and sold to procure coin of
the realm to pay the royal Army. The character
of the few undergraduates who still pursued their
studies was far from exemplary. Here Stoughton
calls in his Oxford historian to verify this charge,
whose partial pen he opines would never have
drawn the description he gives did not truth
compel him to it. Drunkenness, debauchery, gam-
ing, profanity, the writing of ribald songs and

---

[1] " Spiritual Heroes," Chap. VII., p. 184.

ballads, were the daily occupation of the student class, while the most Christian King held his court at Oxford. He looks back with a pained feeling of regret to those days when the University shone with the brightest external glory, numbering her four thousand residents, many of them radiant in costly doublets and goodly apparel, perfumed with odours from the East. Stoughton, however, catches him up by producing documentary evidence that the morals of the students, during the siege, were little more than a continuation of the habits prevalent amongst the glittering four thousand of this earlier period. " I find," he writes, " in the autobiography of Arthur Wilson, a student there in 1630, the following statement " :

" That which was most burdensome to me in this my retirement was the debauchery of the University. For the most eminent scholars of the town, specially of St. John's College, being of my acquaintance, did look upon me with such endearments as took the name of civilities, yet days and nights could witness our madness, and I must confess, the whole time of my life besides did never so much transport me with drinking as that short time I lived at Oxford, and that with some of the gravest bachelors of Divinity there." " Such," adds Stoughton, let us hope without any touch of malice, " was Prelatical Oxford."

Many and great were the changes made, some of them far from wise and wholly unnecessary, when " drab coloured " Puritanism assumed control. On the other hand the reformation of morals, resulting from Puritan rule of the most drastic kind, is worthy of the highest praise and reflects great honour on those who effected it. If dour Presbyterianism abolished the liturgy and the surplice, silenced the organs in most of the chapels, and set up a doleful Scotch precentor to lead the congregation in singing metrical psalms of inordinate length and dullness; if theatres were closed and the amusements of former times prohibited, another change appeared, " truly beautiful in the eyes of those who supremely value the interests of morality and religion." " The very enemies," writes Neale,[1] " of the new heads of colleges have confessed that they were severe in the government of their several houses; that they kept more than a common watch over the morals of the students, and obliged them to use exact compliance with their statutes. The professors were indefatigable in instructing their pupils both in public and in private; religion flourished more than before; drunkenness, oaths and profanation of the Lord's day were banished; strict piety and profession of religion were in fashion."

It is only just to observe, in passing, that piety of this character is no necessary adjunct of the severe Presbyterianism which at this time dominated Oxford, nor would Stoughton or Neale suggest that profanity had any necessary connection with prelacy. The very names of Usher and Andrewes, of Taylor and Herbert would refute such an assumption. The proper conclusion to draw, from the facts here recorded, is

---

[1] " History of the Puritans," Vol. III., p. 473.

that Puritanism came at this time as a great and
necessary purging and cleansing influence, acting
on the whole of our national life with an effect
which, though weakening from time to time, has
proved permanent, and which is likely to be felt
again, with augmented force, to save us in the
evil hour of materialism.

The mistaken idea that Puritanism is necessarily
at war with literature and the fine arts has already
been dealt with. It is, however, a charge which
might be preferred with some justice against
the Presbyterian form of Puritanism in those days.
" Good men," exclaims Stoughton, " they did not
seem as if they could distinguish between art and
its abuse, and because they saw it made subser-
vient to superstition, they were for destroying its
most exquisite monuments." This attitude of
mind is probably responsible for the common belief
that all the havoc wrought upon our ancient
churches is the work of Puritan iconoclasts. They
certainly did not spare objects which they regarded
as ministering to idolatry ; resembling in this
respect the action of some of those brothers of St.
Francis which we have referred to, and the primitive Christians who saw in the temples of Rome
nests of idolatry, reeking with impurities, but
which the modern traveller regards with admiration as the remains of classic genius. We would,
however, be doing a grave injustice to the seventeenth century, and the great men whose acts
made it famous, if we accepted without question
all the exaggerated descriptions of the destruction
of works of art said to have been done during the

civil wars. " It is a common error," observes a
writer in the Archæological Journal,[1] " with
ignorant persons to ascribe most of the mischiefs
from which churches have suffered in the deface-
ment of monuments, or the abstraction of brasses,
to the period of the Great Rebellion. Scarce a
parish clerk is found who, in pointing out some
mutilated figure, or some slab robbed of its effigy,
does not lay the blame on Cromwell's soldiers.
The Puritan faction, who overthrew for a time
altar and throne, have sins enough to answer for
without the addition of those which belong to a
later period."

Much more might be said on this point, and
proof adduced in confirmation of the entire justice
and truthfulness of this last extract, from a writer,
be it observed, who holds no brief for the Puritans ;
but matters of greater moment call for our consideration. The Independent section never took
precisely the same view as the Presbyterian of
spectacular display in dress, ornament, or ceremonial. When Fairfax and Cromwell visited
Oxford, in 1649, it was quite agreeable to them
that some of the grand ceremonial of the former
days should mark the occasion. Some of the
points in Cromwell's speech during this visit
deserve to be remembered, chiefly his remark to
the authorities of the University that " he and his
companions were well aware that no Commonwealth
could flourish without learning, and that whatever the world said to the contrary, they meant
to encourage it, and were so far from abstracting

---

[1] Arch. Journal, Vol. II., p. 244, quoted by Stoughton.

any of their means, that they proposed to add
more ; " a pledge which was faithfully kept. On
the death of the Earl of Pembroke, Cromwell was
appointed Chancellor of Oxford, a post long afterwards filled by another great soldier, the Duke of
Wellington, and proved himself a cordial patron
of learning and the fine arts. He saved the
beautiful windows of King's College, Cambridge,
from spoliation, guarded Hampton Court and
Windsor Castle with a jealous care, made good an
unfulfilled promise of King Charles to Glasgow
University out of his privy purse, attempted the
founding of the University of Durham in 1657, a
project cut short by his death, and bestowed upon
Oxford sundry valuable gifts, amongst them being
twenty-five ancient manuscripts, of which the
greater part were Greek. " But the best service
he rendered to the University," writes Stoughton,
" was the appointment of Dr. John Owen, Dean
of Christ Church, to the Vice-Chancellorship."

Owen being an Independent, naturally enough
there came, in his time, some relaxation of
Presbyterian preciseness and intolerance. In a
work by one Bastwick, a Presbyterian, the luxu-
rious costumes of the Independents are inveighed
against with much vehemence. " You shall
find there," he says, " the only gallants in the
world ; with cuffs, and those great ones at their
very heels, and with more silver and gold upon
their clothes and at their heels—for these upstarts
must have silver spurs—than many great and
honourable personages have in their purses."
Owen himself was not above a touch of splendour

in his attire, though it would appear he merely dressed as an ordinary well-groomed gentleman of the period. At the same time there was under his rule no relaxation of morals or of severe study. He devoted himself to University reforms, the promotion of sound learning, and especially to the introduction of such studies as would fit young men of serious minds to become diligent ministers of religion. He anticipated the efforts of the progressive party of future years by his attempt to abolish the use of unnecessary oaths on taking office and other occasions.

Amongst the contemporaries of Owen were men of real eminence. Thomas Goodwin, "the atlas of Independency," presided at Magdalen. Charnock, the author of "The Divine Attributes," was fellow of New College. Greenwood, described by Neale as "a profound scholar and divine," and by Wood as "a severe and good Governor," was president of Brazenose ; Staunton, "the walking Bible Concordance," president of Corpus, under whom was educated Joseph Alleine, an author well-known to later Evangelicals by his book "A Call to the Unconverted." Dr. Joshua Hoyle had been moved from a Divinity Professorship in Trinity College, Dublin, to the Headship of University. His knowledge of the Roman controversy had probably not been surpassed until the coming of the great Provost Salmon of Dublin. When Wilkins, brother-in-law to Cromwell, presided at Wadham the foundation of the Royal Society was laid by the distinguished scholars who assembled there, in the large room over the gateway, to discuss mathematical problems. In those days Oxford numbered amongst its students John Locke, the future philosopher ; Penn the wise and politic Quaker ; South the distinguished preacher, so pleasantly introduced into the " Spectator " in Addison's delightful sketches of Sir Roger.

Enough, we hope, has been said to prove that though the Puritan rulers of Oxford have left no great works to posterity ; produced no liturgiologist like Cranmer, no theologian like Hooker, no philosopher like Butler, the establishment of law and order in all the Colleges of the University, of industry and diligence in the pursuit of learning, of better manners and of habits of piety amongst undergraduates, may fairly be set against these other attainments, as, in the long run, of far greater advantage than a reputation for brilliancy.

But we need not allow the case against them on the score of learning to go by default. Baxter, Owen, Howe, Charnock, prolix and diffuse as all of them are at times, will in some of their works bear comparison with the best of the Anglican divines. In polite literature also the party attained some real excellence. Passages from Harrington and Marvel[1] may be read with as much pleasure as the charming conceits of Vaughan, Crawshaw or Herbert. Puritan aspirants to literary renown were accustomed to meet in those days in a

---

[1] Chambers' " Cylopædia of English Literature," Vol. I., p. 284.

literary conclave at the Turk's Head in Palace Yard, crossing swords with the choicest wits of the day in a fashion that would have been grateful to the soul of Johnson. Waller, by no means a choice specimen of Puritanism in some passages of his life, was endowed with poetic talent of a very high order. True, there was no successor to Milton in the ranks of Puritanism, but the Anglo-Catholic poets would not be shamed by the accession of George Withers to theirs. Herrick or Crashaw might have written those exquisite lines of his, in praise of his muse :

> " By the murmur of a spring,
> Or the least bough's rusteling,
> By a daisy, whose leaves spread,
> Shut when Titan goes to bed ;
> Or a shady bush or tree—
> She could more infuse in me,
> Than all nature's beauties can
> In some other wiser man."

It is pleasant, too, in days when controversy ran high and hard words were uttered on both sides, to see the little group of searchers after truth, that nucleus of the Royal Society of which mention has been made, " putting aside political and theological topics of debate, by which the kingdom had been divided and convulsed . . . . to discourse of the circulation of the blood, the valves of the veins, the lymphatic vessels, the Copernican hypothesis, and a number of other scientific subjects."[1]

---

[1] Stoughton, " Spiritual Heroes," p. 217.

But these days of peace and order have an end. Owen, Cromwell, and Puritan ascendency at the Universities pass. We have noted Pepys's remark on Cambridge. Let us hear Neale on Oxford after the Restoration. " The University was no less corrupt (than the Court) ; there was a general licentiousness of manners amongst the students ; the sermons of the younger divines were filled with encomiums upon the Church and satire against the Nonconformists ; the Evangelical doctrines of repentance, faith, charity and practical religion were out of fashion. The speeches and panegyrics pronounced by orators and *terrae filius* (sic) on public occasions were scurrilous, and little less than blasphemous."

For all this Puritanism was not dead. It was for the time silenced and thrust into the back ground, but, a hundred years afterwards, the Wesleys found a few kindred spirits at Oxford, ready to foregather with them in religious exercises of a high-church complexion and a decidedly Puritan spirit, and, somewhat later, Charles Simeon bore down the opposition of town and gown to the Evangelical doctrines which he taught from the pulpit of Holy Trinity, Cambridge. Since those days Puritanism has maintained itself as a great force in Cambridge, and, though less strong at the other University, it has never failed of a consider able following amongst the *alumni*, and holds, at the present, an influential position, with the respect and goodwill of many who do not share its opinions ; while at " that small but excellent

University of Dublin "—to quote Bishop Jeremy Taylor's description of it—Puritanism has been supreme, practically, since the time of the illustrious Usher.

CHAPTER XXII

THE Press as we know it is a modern institution. In America its audacity takes away our breath. In England it cannot complain of restrictions. On the whole in both countries it has a high opinion of itself, though possibly it is not nearly so powerful in actual fact as in profession. Nor can it be said that its extraordinary popularity is wholly good. The Newspaper man, whether producer or client, is rarely Bacon's full man. The hasty journalism of our times does not compare advantageously with the pamphlet journalism of the Stuart and Commonwealth periods as a literary product. In the Library of Viscount Clifden, at Lanhydrock, a considerable number of such pamphlets may be seen neatly bound and occupying almost a whole shelf; and a reader opening any of them at random may be sure of finding sound argument, accurate information, trenchant language, whatever the writer's point of view may be. The principal writers of those days, Royalists and Roundheads, knew their subjects and reasoned with great dexterity, and the reader who was prudent and just enough to read both sides, could see each case fairly and see it whole. It is to be feared that the very super-abundance of our present day newspapers and journals satiate rather than inform the mind; we can hardly see the wood for the trees, and the mind which draws its knowledge chiefly from the daily papers does not retain it long. Such knowledge at the best is but scrappy, while the newspaper habit disinclines the constant reader from more serious study, and what is of far greater moment, from serious thinking. The vast majority of Englishmen allow the newspaper to do their thinking for them. It saves trouble, but it is on the whole as much a disservice as a help. Say what we will, however, the Britisher will have his morning and evening paper and this being the case it is perhaps wise to restrict its liberty as little as possible.

The Anglo-Saxon in England or America would kill by pure ridicule, if by no other way, the kind of press oversight and censorship which prevailed in Russia under the Czars and in Germany under the Hohenzollerns. Yet there was a time when the censorship in England was not only rigorous but penal beyond justification, as poor Prynne, with his amputated ears, learned to his cost. King, Parliament, Presbyterian and Independent, all tried their hands in turn one time or another, in restraining the free expression of opinion. It is true opinion was often expressed with a freedom that exceeded the limits of decency, but as the writer could fairly estimate the risk, and was willing to hazard it, we may spare some admiration for his temerity, while declining to approve his violence. But in the long run it was found as impossible to tune the Press as the Bishops or the Presbyterian party had found it impossible to tune the pulpits. Above all the Parliament whose *raison d'être* was the promotion of liberty must have felt the task of abridging liberty inconsistent. Neale puts the case for the Parliament very fairly, pointing out the provocations of the malignants and others which not only affected the dignity of the House, a small thing if unpleasant, but aimed at the subversion of the Government and the taking " off the affections of the people from it." This was in 1649, but at an earlier period, 1643, an order was issued, mainly through Presbyterian influence, that all printing presses should be licensed and all printed matter submitted to a Censor before publication. There is little doubt that so far as the Presbyterian party—at this time by far the strongest party in Parliament — was concerned the order was directed chiefly against Milton, whose tracts on divorce had roused Presbyterian anger to a white heat. Into the merits of the discussion we need not enter except to observe, in passing, that, to those who regarded the Home as the most essential element in Society, it must have appeared impossible to preserve an ordered social life, in any State, if divorce could be obtained in the easy and free way advocated by Milton. At the same time, anarchical as his views on this and other matters may have been, we have grounds for some degree of gratitude that the unsavoury subject proved the indirect cause of the appearance of the famous *Areopagitica*, probably

Q

the greatest of all his tracts ; a masterpiece of stately English and powerful pleading. It did not succeed, immediately, in its object, for we have seen that six years later a similar order was issued ; and not until 1694 was the censorship of the Press removed ; the era of the revolution bringing to flower many of the seeds sown by Puritan hands.

It is not necessary to claim a high place for the Press as an intellectual or educational agent while upholding its value, and, indeed, its necessity, as an instrument for safeguarding the political and religious liberties of the nation. The Press, however free, can never become a censor in the proper sense of censorship, for that would involve a power of imposing its views by force, but it can be, and frequently is, a wise and powerful critic of governments and ecclesiastical institutions. No freedom-loving people, then, can dispense with a free Press. Its evils are, no doubt, manifold, but, in a Christian country, so long as it abstains from blasphemy and sedition, the greatest good is to be had by leaving it quite unmuzzled. Very few of us would be found willing to commit ourselves to an opinion held in many quarters that the newspaper and the review now fill the place held by the sermon in other days ; for we know by experience that great preachers like Spurgeon, Liddon, John Watson, Ward-Beecher, Philips Brooks, men with a message, will always attract multitudes. The love of eloquence is as strong in us as the love of song ; empty churches most frequently mean bad preachers. Yet the influence of the Press upon our political and religious life is considerable, and most certainly touches depths of society never reached by the pulpit. It is, therefore, matter for congratulation that the chief organs of the daily Press, both in England and America, are on the side of Christian morality, while wisely abstaining from siding with religious parties ; and that on questions of politics the expression of opinion is generally candid and disinterested, according to the organ's point of view, though occasionally giving rise to a suspicion that Esau's hands and Jacob's voice are still often found in conjunction, for no worthier object than Jacob had.

The usefulness of a free Press and unlicensed printing being admitted, it will repay us to look back to the source of these benefits, and hear how the greatest of Puritans voiced the claim of his country for them half a century before they were granted. Milton advances his claim with great caution, acknowledging the right and the duty of the State to interfere in matters which affect its own interest and the public good. Seditious and blasphemous publications may rightly be suppressed and their authors punished, but the *Areopagitica* is nevertheless a clarion call to free men to speak freely in a free State, a quotation from " Euripides " asking the question, " What can be juster in a State than this ? " appropriately appearing on the title page.

He professes that in asking so much there is " nothing new or insolent " in the demand, for is he not on the side of the champions in old Greece in so doing ? He tells the Lords and Commons, " the meek demeanour " of whose " civill and

gentle greatness " he admires, that he is assured
how much better they " esteem it to imitate the
old and elegant humanity of Greece than the
barbarick pride of Hunnish and Norwegian stateli-
ness," and appeals for justification of his own and
their positions, to those ages " to whose polite
wisdom and letters we owe that we are not yet
Gothes and Jutlanders." He fears that the order
to allow no book or pamphlet to appear unless
first approved and licensed may, amongst other
things, do grave injury to learning " by hindering
and cropping the discovery that might bee yet
further made both in religion and civill wisdom."
Here we have the true Baconian and modern spirit,
that will have truth, cost what it may. " As good,"
he proceeds, " kill a man as kill a good booke ;
who kills a man kills a reasonable spirit, God's
image ; but he who destroys a good booke, kills
reason itself, kills the image of God, as it were, in
the eye." The tract throughout is an interesting
illustration of the Puritan view that religion and
politics may not be separated, that civil and
religious liberty go hand in hand. To attempt any
description, therefore, of Puritan character or
Puritan influence, with either of these principles
left out, must end in failure. We cannot conceive
of a Puritan of those times with whom interest in
the State fell short of his interest in religion, or
whose interest in religion did not demand of him,
by the very nature of his profession, the utmost
solicitude for the welfare of the State. His
political outlook was determined by his view of
religion. Now, as regards the latter, the greatest

lesson Puritanism and the English Reformation taught us is the openness of approach to God. The veil is rent and the way into the holiest is free to the humblest believer. Thus the occupation of the Confessor is gone. Priest or prelate is no nearer the mercy seat than the swain who ploughs the field. What is man's right becomes man's duty; he must neither invite nor permit intrusion between himself and God. There is no softness about a religion of this type; it is essentially virile; the soul learns to know and to hold direct communion with its Almighty Creator, nothing between; and the fight with evil for each of us is in the open and single-handed, a personal faith in the great Deliverer, best gift of all, sustaining us. "I cannot praise," writes Milton in this tract, "a fugitive and cloister'd virtue, unexercised and unbreath'd, that never sallies out and sees her adversary, but slinks out of the race." It is not difficult to form a conception of the kind of politician such a view of religion would produce. He would be one who would judge of questions, and of all propositions relating to them, on their merits; who would bind his conscience to no man; who would vote and act according to the best of his judgment; breathing the air of a free faith he would claim all the privileges of a free man. A little reflection will teach us that all this is better in theory than it has proved in practice. It was fortunate for Puritanism that it did not carry all Milton's proposals to their logical conclusion. Great as the man was, his idea of liberty, which came practically to " hands off everything," is quite unworkable in a world of imperfect beings. As things turned out, though this extreme view did not prevail, the right of private judgment claimed and exercised by the Sectaries came near to ruining the Commonwealth, and so perplexed and harassed the Protector that, in order to preserve liberty, he felt compelled for the moment to destroy liberty, and take the whole control of the State into his own hands.[1] It is conceivable that, if all men had in them such a righteous spirit as Milton's, we might dispense with laws and churches and suffer every man to do what seemed right in his own eyes. He, at all events, never doubted that, with absolute freedom, right would in the long run always prevail over wrong. " Though all the winds of doctrine were let loose to play upon the earth, so Truth be in the field, we do, ingloriously, by licensing and prohibiting, to misdoubt her strength. Let her and falsehood grapple. Who ever knew truth put to the worse in a free and open encounter ? " " For who knows not," he proceeds, " that Truth is strong, next to the Almighty ? She needs no policies, no stratagems, no licensings, to make her victorious ; those are the shifts and the defences that error uses against her power ; give her but room, and do not bind her when she sleeps." Such are Milton's views on the liberty of printing, and may be regarded as expressing the Puritan view of liberty in general. Somewhat diluted, for experience has taught us that some restraint of individual freedom is necessary, they are the principles which govern

---

[1] De Rapin, " History of England " XIII. p. 80.

men in every country and dominion where the English language is spoken and English law, or law which approximates to it, is in force. In his travels abroad, especially in Italy, where he " sat among their learned men," he had heard England praised as " a place of philosophic freedom," beyond, as Milton thought, its merits ; yet he took it as a pledge of future happiness, and his view of England, rising and expanding under the influence of generous laws and free institutions, reads like the utterance of an inspired prophet. " Methinks," he writes, " I see in my mind a noble and puissant nation rousing herself like a strong man after sleep, and shaking her invincible locks ; methinks I see her as an eagle mewing her mighty youth, and kindling her undazzled eyes, at the full midday beam ; purging and unsealing her long-abused sight at the fountain itself of heavenly radiance ; while the whole noise of timorous and flocking birds, with those also that love the twilight, flutter about amazed at what she means."

This Puritan was no Little Englander, nor was Cromwell. Two hundred and seventy years after Milton wrote this eloquent passage, England, with a population eight times larger than in Milton's day, with wealth and material resources he never dreamed of, and having stretched out her branches to the sea and " hatched the American Eagle," as well as many a mighty State all her own, undertakes the task, with the subsequent aid of that generous and great Republic, of saving France from destruction and the world from bondage. No England, but such an England as Milton visualised, and for whose expansion Cromwell fought, could have ventured on so great an enterprise. It was Milton's England, "kindling her undazzled eyes at the full mid-day beam," standing by the side of France, and aided by Puritan America, that stayed the fury and broke the power of the mightiest military forces Europe ever saw. And so has the Puritan prophet's vision come true. "God grant our greatness may not fail through craven fear of being great."

CHAPTER XXIII

PURITANISM IN THE TWENTIETH CENTURY

SOME of our most reputable historians head their pages with the words "the decline of Puritanism," and an English Church authority informs his readers that Charles Simeon was the last of the Evangelicals. Not to be beaten, the humorous "Phil May" gives an amusing sketch of an elderly maiden aunt receiving on her birthday the felicitations of her two nephews, who came to drink her health. "You," she murmurs, in a melancholy voice, "dear boys, have a long and happy future before you, but as for me the joy of life is departed. I am the last of the Smiths,"

"Puritanism," writes Lord Morley, "threw out an extreme left with a hundred offshoots of its own," an observation much nearer the truth than the end of either the Smiths or the Puritans. Some of those offshoots seem very unlike the parent stem, especially those of a political character, yet, as the oak sleeps in the acorn, the most disturbing political movements, the most revolutionary changes the country has experienced, during the last hundred years, can be amply justified by a reference to the doctrines preached by Knox in Scotland, by Owen and others in England, and by Hampden and Pym in the Commons.

Indeed, a higher ancestry may be claimed for them, for Puritanism, breaking free from the feudal conception of society, restored to us the forgotten Pauline teaching that the Creator has made of one blood all nations of men to dwell on the earth. The middle class trader or manufacturer who took his turn at preaching in chapel on Sunday and was careful to tell the working men present that we are all equal in the sight of God, ought not to have been shocked—though he most certainly was shocked, at the outbreak of Chartism. For Chartism simply was a claim for equality of treatment, and the expression of a nation's bitter disappointment at the barren results of the Reform Act of 1832. Again, if capital withheld from the worker more than was meet, it is not surprising that the man who had learned in his roadside chapel that " the earth had been given to the children of men," set himself with his fellows to form a Trades Union as the shortest road to getting his fair share of it. The claims of Labour, often just, often unreasonable, sometimes impossible and rarely polite, can be explained by the fact that through Puritanism the labouring man found himself ; he counted for something ; he was a man, no less than the Cabinet Minister or the judge. This may not be the true explanation, but it must serve until a better is found. Labour is now so much alive, has so fully developed its nervous system, that some of our Churches are expunging from their hymn books the lines " the rich man in his castle, the poor man at his gate, God made them high and lowly and ordered their estate," lest Labour should take offence, or it may be from the far better feeling that such comparisons are unsuitable in a place where " rich and poor meet together," the Lord being the Maker of them all. We shall not therefore be very wide of the mark in attributing to Puritanism the credit or the blame of having had, at all events, some part in the creation of this new spirit in Labour and consequently in the movements which arose out of it. " For the last two hundred years," writes J. R. Green, " England has been doing little more than carrying out, in a slow and tentative way, the scheme of political and religious reform which the Army propounded at the close of the civil war."[1] The spirit of this scheme may be gathered from a passage in Cromwell's letter to Lenthall, Speaker in the Long Parliament, after the battle of Dunbar, where his exhausted army of eleven thousand overwhelmed a Scotch army under Leslie of double that number. He urges upon Lenthall the recognition of the Army, "for they are the chariots and horsemen of Israel," and then proceeds to offer counsel to the Parliament. " Disown yourselves," he says, " but own your authority ; and improve it to curb the proud and the insolent, such as would disturb the tranquility of England, though under what specious pretences soever. Relieve the oppressed, hear the groans of the poor prisoners in England. Be pleased to reform the abuses of all professions ; and if there be anyone that makes many poor to make a few rich, that suits not a Commonwealth."

---

[1] Green's " History of the English People," VII. p. 251.

There is hardly a claim for redress that has been put forward by any section of the population since 1650, more especially by Labour, which may not be covered and justified by this counsel ; and in short we may say that the essence of the whole political programme of the Clapham Sect, and the so-called humanity-mongers, is contained in these few sentences.

Two important movements within the English Church in more recent times have not been without their effect on Puritanism on its religious side. We have already called attention to the Royal Society, and to such writers as Bacon, Locke and Hobbes. The new spirit generated by thinkers of this class may account for the rise of a small but interesting party about the middle of the seventeenth century, known as the Cambridge Platonists, of whom Whichcote was perhaps the greatest. They maintained, very justly it would seem, that Christianity must have not only its historical and emotional, but also a philosophical basis, and proceeded to co-ordinate the religious and the philosophical positions. They took Plato as their master, hence the title Platonists, but as—according to a witty paradox—" no one has ever understood Plato but Aristotle, and he did not," the party failed to make much headway. Nevertheless it was on the side of tolerance, in favour of a comprehensive national Church—inclusive not exclusive—demanded that tradition must commend itself to reason ; and might have numbered Arnold and Whately amongst its later disciples.

The other movement, known as Tractarianism,

from the attempt to propagate its principles by
the issue of tracts, arose about 1833, and aimed at
strengthening the position of the English Church
and recovering its conception of a corporate life,
which had been somewhat lost sight of in the
emphasis which the Evangelical revival had laid
upon the individual. These objects were highly
praiseworthy, but the party at once adopted the
Cyprianic view of the Church and its ministry,
ignored the fact that the English Church was
frankly Erastian, regarded Lutherans and Nonconformists as schismatics, raised again in acute
form the vexatious vestment question, and claimed
that the Church Catholic included only the three
branches, the Roman, the Eastern and the Anglican;
and thus very soon came into collision with men of
broader minds. Its usefulness was further im-
paired by attacks on Dr. Jowett of Balliol College,
and a clergyman named Gorham in the Diocese of
Exeter, from which it appeared that it aimed at
silencing or forcing out of the Church all who refused
to accept its somewhat unusual interpretations of
certain doctrines. "At its best," wrote Professor
Dowden, "the Church of England has been of the
nature of a federal union between groups of believers in a common Christianity, whose diverging
opinions in detail are wholly incapable of logical
conciliation; at its worst it has attempted to
establish the unity of an idea, a theory, or a system,
and has denied the right of citizenship to its lawful
children."[1] "As a historical fact," he adds,

---

[1] Dowden, "Puritan and Anglican," p. 78. See also
Fawkes' "Church and State in England" (Murray, 1s.).

dealing with those who deny Calvinism a footing in the Church, " the Church of England has been Calvinist, and Arminian, and Latitudinarian, and Evangelical, and Sacramental. Its unity has not been the unity of an idea but that of a living organism." Unfortunately, what Dowden deems the " worst " has been this party's choice ; yet in spite of limitations and a decided reactionary tendency, it has shown signs of vigorous life and has done heroic work in many directions, and having a majority of the clergy in its ranks and a great female following it is probably come to stay. Indeed, so long as it is content to accept a place in the national establishment, and refrains from the attempt to impede the advance of the more liberal and progressive sections, its departure would now be reckoned a loss. The bare statement of this fact shows that Puritanism, without parting with its own principles, has enlarged its borders and proved its capacity for adaptation.

Another movement known as Aestheticism, not directly connected with religion, has also had its effect on Puritanism, though not to the extent of its influence on Tractarianism. Indeed, the latter party is believed to owe much of its popularity, with the more emotional sections of the population, to its foresight in allying itself at an early date with this movement ; for to that circumstance we may attribute in some measure the increased order, decency and cleanliness in our churches, a more ornate ritual in public worship, and, we must add, a feverish desire all over the land to restore the old parish churches, an enterprise attended by some very unhappy results. Zealous young vicars, who had caught the Catholic fever, fell into raptures over rood-screens, Baldachinos, and Lady Chapels ; faculties were easily obtained from benevolent bishops, or not obtained at all, and, with the best will in the world to improve the rustic taste, many of our fine old fanes of prayer were restored beyond recognition, and some of their most interesting features permanently destroyed. Nevertheless the aesthetic movement has been valuable. If it did nothing more it made our places of worship clean and decent. Churches and Chapels present a brighter and more cheerful appearance to the worshipper ; congregations are more orderly and decorous ; many of the accessories of public worship are improved ; while the homes of the middle classes are touched with a delicate and artistic grace, which contrasts favourably with the sombreness and heavy dullness of the Hanoverian period.

It was impossible that Puritanism should remain untouched by changes such as these, which brought both loss and gain. We know not how far mind and character are affected by surroundings, but the cumulative effect of these changes seems to have been a softening of the strong Anglo-Saxon nature, and the rendering of the Celtic portion of the people more pliable, and more susceptible to the influence of passionate rhetoric.

Thus, while the Puritans have been impressing their policies on others, a combination of circumstances has been making impressions on them. Political changes they have met and accepted ; religious changes they can survive, but there is one change which is so seriously impairing their moral force, it may in the end prove their ruin and with them that of England. The amazing prosperity of England as a great trading nation has dulled spiritual sensibility to an alarming degree, and diverted thought from those high ideals which inspired the Christian leaders of the eighteenth century. The nation has made to itself gods of silver and gold. A hundred years ago at the head of nearly every great banking house in the kingdom, a Puritan, most often a Quaker, might be found ; the chairmanships of shipping and railway companies were filled by them ; Puritans were tea merchants, rice merchants, corn and coal merchants ; and the successful small trader in the country town was frequently of the same persuasion. Yet rotten ships went to sea, heavily insured, and never returned ; great banking houses came crashing down, involving a confiding public in financial ruin, and we have seen with what difficulty Wilberforce and others overcame the opposition of their Puritan friends to the abolition of the Slave Trade, and how Puritans opposed Lord Ashley when fighting the battle of women and young children. Nor can we claim that the small tradesman has always been above reproach, as the well-known story of Dr. Adam Clark, when a draper's apprentice, proves. In America the state of things was even worse than in England. The orgy of the New York Stock Exchange ; the glaring unfairness and tyranny of the " big " Trusts ; the Tammany " Boss," are felt by the best type of American to be the running sores of his country. Need we wonder that an observer of all this should say that " dishonesty in trade has been the Achilles' heel of Puritanism ? " It is, of course, unnecessary to say that amidst all this commercial growth and the allurement of riches a noble integrity has been maintained by a large body of merchants and traders in both countries ; at the same time it cannot be denied that our prosperity has been accompanied by a serious weakening of the Puritan spirit of righteousness. Parliament is generous, but at other people's expense ; the charge has been made that honours are sold by political parties like wares over a shop counter ; that expediency and not principle is the guide of statesmen. Much of this may be idle rumour, but it is no idle rumour that far and wide the masses are turning away from religion of every type, while high and low make Sunday a day of riot and pleasure. If Puritanism has been the salt of English social life, the salt, for the moment, has lost its saltness. England's greatest need today is not a great statesman—admittedly a desideratum—but a great Apostle. A twentieth century Wesley, a new Puritan, with a message suited to the age and with a key to England's heart would set us right in Church and State ; since we may not doubt that a nation standing right with God could not fail to be right with man. And that is the root idea of Puritanism in both of its aspects, the political and the religious. Such favours once were ours, and should be ours again ; for Puritanism never dies. It has once and again slumbered or suffered temporary eclipse, but only to burst out again " kindling its undazzled eyes." " The

R

future," said Bishop Wilberforce, "is but history prolonged, the past as it were lifted up and thrust out again before us "; and so the lovers and friends of England and of America may indulge the hope that this great movement, cleansed of its imperfections, will return to us as an abiding influence for good, welcomed by all, purifying both our political and our ecclesiastical institutions.

In the army of the New Model Cromwell would have none but Godly men, and with them the cause of freedom prevailed. In the judgment of many, Puritanism is the only power that can take Cromwell's place, on a vaster scale, in turning the whole nation into an army of the new model, for the creation of a prosperous England at peace with itself. But to this end modern Puritanism has much to learn and some things to forget. It must forget old enmities and causes of strife, and it must learn to unite all its forces. Happily prelacy is no longer "the accursed thing" to devout Free Churchmen, and the Apostolic labours of the Free Churches have wrought a great and welcome change in the feelings of prelacy towards them. The World Missionary Conference at Edinburgh, in 1910, proved a great educator. We have found that we are nearer to each other than we had ever thought since good sense began to take the place of criticism —"a beam in darkness, let it grow." On the Political side we have had our coalition; not, indeed, a brilliant success, but solidly good in principle; for politicians, as well as theologians, have meaningless shibboleths and idols of the cave. We are learning to drop the shibboleths, which, if followed by a holocaust of the idols, would be as life from the dead for political England. A Christian Church co-extensive with the Empire is a fair dream, not yet realisable. Cranmer's gentleness, Laud's dragooning, Arnold's reasoning have in turn failed ; but a union of Christian forces is now possible, and its accomplishment falls to the lot of the Puritan parties in all the Churches ; for they alone have that fulness of sympathy and knowledge which the occasion demands. From such a union much may be hoped, in winning the masses to a recognition of essential Christianity, in reconciling the two great forces, capital and labour, on which our material existence depends, and in permeating our politics with that spirit of righteousness, for the promotion of which Puritanism came into existence, and which, if once recovered, must go far to make an end of all dishonesties and all corruptions in " this State of England."

Here then is the task awaiting Puritanism. Will it fail, or will it, by a sacrifice of ease and fortune and worldly honours, " outshine the glory of its dawn in the splendour of its noon ? "

INDEX

Vaughan, Henry, hymns, 74.
Venables, Commander, 57.
Venn, John, 7, 182.
Virginia, 99, 107, 109.
Voluntaryism, 42.

Wade, C.E., estimate of Pym, 28.
Wakeman, H., "History of the Church of England," 184.
Wales, Prince of, 181.
Walker, Samuel, ministry, 183, 185.
Waller, Edmund, 224.
Ward, Mrs. Humphry, "Robert Elsmere," 15.
Ward-Beecher, Henry, sermons, 230.
Watson, John, sermons, 230.
Wellington, Duke of, character of his administration, 52; Chancellor of Oxford, 221.
Welsh Church, disendowment, 36.
Wentworth, Thomas, 17; apostacy, 23, 80.
Wesley, Charles, hymns, 173.
Wesley, John, Journal, viii, 170; hymn-book, 38; influence of his teaching, 136, 165; religious views, 169, 171; parents, 170; mode of life, 170, 172; mission to Georgia, 170; a "legalist," 171; preaching, 172;

relation to the Church of England, 173; views on the Apostolic succession, 174; uncompromising Arminian, 178; political views, 178.
Wesleyanism, separation from the Church, 177.
Weston, Agnes, "Sailors' Rests," 200.
Whately, Archbishop, 240.
Whichcote, Benjamin, 140.
Whigs, 180.
Whitfield, George, first leader of the Evangelical party, 179; field-sermons, 181, eloquence, 182.
Whitman, Walt, 104; "Democratic Vistas," 110.
Whittier, John, 104.
Wilberforce, Bishop, 246.
Wilberforce, William, 187; work in the abolition of the Slave Trade, 189, 204, 244.
William III., King, 50.
Wilson, Arthur, on the condition of Oxford University, 217.
Withers, George, lines of, 224.
Wood, Anthony, "Annals of the University," 216.
Woolman, Journal of John, 108.
Working classes, condition, 114.
World Missionary Conference, at Edinburgh, 246.
Wyclif, John, teaching, 136, 144.